THE STRATEGIC BUSINESS OF YOU

A PERSONAL MANAGEMENT GUIDE FOR A MEANINGFUL LIFE

DR. DAFNE TORO

Ballast Books, LLC
www.ballastbooks.com

ISBN: 978-1-962202-19-0
Library of Congress Control Number: 2023921553

Printed in the United States of America

Published by Ballast Books
West Palm Beach, Florida
www.ballastbooks.com

For more information, bulk orders, appearances, or speaking requests,
please email: info@ballastbooks.com
or thestrategicbusinessofyou@gmail.com.

To my beloved husband and much-loved son.

TABLE OF CONTENTS

INTRODUCTION

I had a strange feeling. My husband and I were on a crowded bus on our way back to our hotel after a fully packed vacation day. During one of our breaks, I read about a dangerous virus that was working its way through an important business location in Asia.

Due to the high flow of people, I was concerned about the potential of the virus spreading. I'd kept up with headlines about viruses before, but this felt different. My husband looked at me.

"Honey, don't worry. Everything will be fine," he said.

Neither of us knew that our world was about to change.

The ravage of a pandemic was something unimaginable for this generation. The year 2020 was one of the worst years on record for the world economy and modern society. But no economic indicator compares with the number of lives claimed by the virus. More than six million lives were lost in this pandemic.

The pandemic forced me to rethink aspects of life, which at times meant surrendering to fear, loneliness, and uncertainty. For starters, it helped me to better conceptualize an idea for a new approach to life management, which had begun taking shape years before. It also helped me realize how privileged I was throughout that time and helped reinforce for me that life is a gift, not a given.

I am not alone. The last few years have brought a lot of change and forced many people to rethink their lives, how they spend their time, and their relationships. Many people quit their jobs; others got divorced.

While it became more evident in recent years, the desire to change to a better state is something I had seen in people years before the pandemic. Often, crises push us to act, but not necessarily in the right direction. Many of us just don't know where to start and feel stuck with no clear path. I've been there before—longing for change, wanting something better—but I didn't know how. Daily life absorbed me and clouded my vision of the future. Not having a clear structure prevented me from creating the foundation for the balanced life I had once envisioned.

What the pandemic helped me and many other people understand more than ever was the value of living a meaningful life. I decided to focus on what really mattered, and I wanted to develop a replicable process for doing so. I started to connect the dots to create the Life Management Approach (LMA), a new mindset that allowed me to understand the value and the fragility of our existence; how we maximize our resources; the value of time and sharing; and, in the end, how we can do our best in this journey called life. What I realized through this process changed my life, and I am sure that it can change yours.

Just as companies have strategies to pursue and achieve goals, individuals can use a similar approach to move to a better state in their lives. The Life Management Approach helps to establish a thought structure as a strategy to set up what is really important for a balanced and meaningful life.

After spending years studying businesses and organizations, as well as how individuals apply strategies and theories to achieve a common goal, I started to see a similar dynamic in my personal life. The management approach I learned about in books and practiced in the corporate world started to make sense in my personal life as well. A lot of us wear many hats in life due to different circumstances. That's fine—that's life. The challenge is to fulfill all the roles and demands of daily life in a balanced and meaningful way.

As a PhD in business, wife, mother, daughter, sister, and strategic business manager, I realized that there are a lot of business concepts and theories that we can connect to our personal lives to help us make better decisions, maximize our strengths, manage adversity, and more. Some of these theories have been applied by organizations for years to improve their performance and achieve their goals.

The Life Management Approach is a framework for developing personal strategic thinking to make better decisions, navigate adversity, manage conflicts, and maximize personal resources. Some of the concepts are more focused on personal relationships or career improvement, while others are more oriented to having a better thought structure and balance between roles. The concepts are integrated with the goal of achieving better stability and an overall higher level of harmony, self-realization, and joy.

Creating change often requires us to see and think about things in a different way. A new thought structure sets the foundation for actions. Those actions do not have to be radical or giant, but they are actions with purpose and aim to create real change.

The Life Management Approach outlines four main pillars of well-being that we should pay attention to: physical, emotional, spiritual, and financial. These pillars are the keys to balance, harmony, and inner peace, which, when combined, equal success. How can you address the four pillars? Through the allocation of your personal resources (time, energy, and money). Like business organizations, we, too, have limited resources. Maximizing and aligning the most important resources for the good of the four pillars will lead to a better life state. Problems in life will not always correlate one-to-one with these pillars, but the framework I am sharing helps in the daily challenges and overall life decisions.

Life cannot be treated as a product, company, or asset. However, it is definitely our job and responsibility to determine how we conduct our life. In business school, I learned theories to understand enterprise issues. Those theories can be applied to case studies and therefore can help to solve—and sometimes prevent—issues and achieve results. In the following chapters, we will go over concepts that have previously been applied to business and economic theories and learn how to integrate them into your personal life.

Similar to business, the LMA can be applied to your personal life through a formula: theory + decision = action.

School didn't teach us how to manage and make money, how to invest, how to self-motivate, or how to have a growth-mindset approach. It didn't teach us how to structure our life, how to manage decision-making, or how to face adversity. As a professional certified life coach, I have used the Life Management Approach to fill this gap. To date, I have helped many people develop more meaningful lives using the concepts in this book. I hope the next chapters offer you some helpful ideas on these fundamental topics of our lives.

The Life Management Approach
What it IS and what it IS NOT about

✓		✗	
✓	Reinvention	✗	Living in a Bubble
✓	Structured Thought Process	✗	Throw-Away Culture
✓	Values-Added Choices	✗	Idealistic Ideas
✓	Simplification	✗	Instant Gratification

If you are looking for the secret to becoming a millionaire, this book is not for you. I will leave that to other experts. And you don't have to study business or management to understand and apply the Life Management Approach. I'll keep it simple.

The Life Management Approach is not a one-size-fits-all strategy. It is a very personal and unique process—as unique as we are. Nor is it a static or one-time overnight process. It requires constant and honest revision. Just as companies are continuously reviewing their plans and results, we must review ours and ensure they are meaningful and healthy. When we do this—and do it with purpose—we can create the fulfilling lives we all desire.

CHAPTER 1

YOUR LIFE, YOUR BUSINESS

Most businesses operate within a management framework. They calculate risk, allocate resources, execute according to a plan, and then evaluate their performance. Throughout my career, I've seen how companies organize themselves and operate under a well-structured framework to achieve a goal. Small, medium, and large businesses have different goals. To achieve those goals, most of them define a strategy, put a plan in place, execute, and then evaluate the results. Each one executes under what they believe is the best for the company. Strategies and plans are aligned to the organization's mission, vision, and core values.

A similar exercise or dynamic occurs in our personal lives. We all must make decisions, measure the risk, execute, evaluate the results, celebrate success, and learn from failure. The LMA pursues a life of balance, harmony, and continuous improvement. Throughout the process, we not only learn from what we've done well, but also from what we got wrong and could have done better.

Commonly, there are two ways to view learning and growth: learning the hard way from our own failures, or learning from others—that is, identifying what we want and don't want by observing the actions of others. This development process requires observation, analysis, and decision-making. Learning from others is not always possible and is not always best.

To grow and be authentic, companies must make their own decisions. Chances to fail always exist, and that's OK. The difference lies in what we do with failure. Do we learn from it and move on? Or are we paralyzed by the fear of failing and do nothing?

The same concept applies to our personal lives. When I was younger, I looked at how some adults lived their lives. Some hated their jobs, stayed in obvious toxic relationships, or had kids they didn't spend quality time with. Bottom line: they met some "social standards," but they were not happy or had completely imbalanced lives. Often, it was not one single factor that contributed to this; these individuals struggled in several aspects of their lives. Though I wasn't able to verbalize it at the time, these adults were living in what I now call "survival mode." They were not happy and fulfilled, and I knew I did not want that for my adult life.

Later in life, I dedicated time to analyzing those cases, and I was able to conceptualize the term "survival mode" and identify some common factors. They were all living one day at a time without a strategy or plan. They blamed others for their situations or failures, expressing how unlucky they had been in life, or how unfair their circumstances were. I do not say this judgmentally. They were not bad people. Some of them were smart and hard workers. They had opportunities. They had tools. But from my observations, their lives were a mess. I identified that, in almost all cases, they did not have a structure or framework. They did not act according to any plan, priorities, or scale of values.

By observing this, I realized that if I didn't want that kind of life, I needed a plan. I needed a path and a framework if I wanted to have a different journey. I had to think differently and make things different. It was then that I began to conceive of a framework, inspired by the strategic thinking involved in business, to achieve a balanced and meaningful life.

Similar to a business startup, we don't achieve things in our personal lives overnight. It takes planning, execution, and revision. It's an overall iterative process to achieve our goals, and that process can be summarized as living through a Life Management Approach. Every day is a gift and an opportunity to improve ourselves. There are a lot of things that we cannot control. However, there are a lot of important aspects that we can control. The quality of our relationships, our habits, how we manage adversity, and how much we share with others are just a few examples of things that we can control and that can make a difference in how we walk this journey.

Adversity is something we cannot control. Everyone will experience adverse events at some point. In fact, adversity and failure are part of life. The difference is how we handle it and, more importantly, what we get out of it. The implementation of LMA thinking does not happen overnight. It takes effort, discipline, and time. You need to train your brain to move toward this framework. In my case, it took years to change my mindset. It is a process of continuous personal evolution. It is not finished, and it will not finish until our last day in this world.

But What Is the Life Management Approach?

In business, the strategic management approach helps organizations make better decisions in the short term and also for the future. It helps to ensure that the organization is contemplating the important variables and potentially impacted areas of the business. It's the same in our personal lives. The LMA is about the structure that leads to reinvention, but this time, not for a company. This time, it's for ourselves. It is a way to organize and conceptualize the information relevant to our decision-making, relying heavily on prioritization and small actions over time.

This framework is not like making a New Year's resolution. It's about developing a different mindset, or a different way to see our journey through this world. We really don't know how long our journey will last, so we must embrace each day as a gift and an opportunity. These personal strategies are translated into daily choices that drive action. Like it or not, choices shape your whole life. That is why it's so important to pay attention to them, no matter how big or small they are. People have different goals in life, and there can be many definitions of success. Independent of individual goals, success is about meaning, happiness, and harmony.

The structure of the LMA focuses on four pillars of well-being: physical, emotional, spiritual, and financial. The first three pillars are at the center, and the fourth supports the first three. Our actions should align with these pillars to keep us healthy and positive and allow us to continue to grow and develop. Through the LMA, we can find balance and harmony, which will then cascade into many factors of daily life. The goal of the LMA is to achieve balance and well-being within each of the four pillars. But don't stop there. Achieving balance helps us to accelerate in life, to move forward, and to be a better version of ourselves.

How Can I Achieve Balance and Well-Being in the Four Pillars?

We can achieve balance and well-being in the four pillars through prioritization. Identify within the four pillars what is really important, and allocate the resources toward that. The Life Management Approach establishes three main resources that we should pay attention to and maximize: **time**, **energy**, and **money**. We all have limited resources, so we should be careful how we spend these three.

Time is unique. It is a resource that does not return. It's what we use to create, heal, love, and share. Minutes, hours, days, years, decades—time forms our story, or our journey, and should be addressed as the precious resource it is through conscientious time management and purpose.

Energy is related to state of mind and is the inner engine to pursue and achieve our goals. It's about the positive or negative energy we receive and give to others. That inner engine can take us backward with negativity and imbalance, making our life equation unsolvable. Or it can take us forward to a life with value-added results. The power of energy directly impacts our spiritual and emotional pillars. That is why it is important to be the custodians of our energy, feeding our hearts and minds with positive and constructive things and rejecting the emotional trash.

Money is the physical resource that allows us to create and share a lot of things. It should not be the driver. The financial pillar and money as a resource is the way to facilitate execution. We should pay attention to it from a resource perspective and not as an indicator of success.

LIFE MANAGEMENT APPROACH

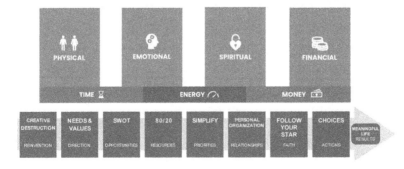

Because everyone is different, there is no single model that works for everything. In the following chapters, we'll see just a few of the theories and concepts that help with the development of a personal LMA. Once we establish the overall strategic mindset through continuous learning, we can integrate other concepts that are more aligned to the current scenario.

Theories and concepts like Schumpeter's creative destruction, Maslow's hierarchy of needs, the SWOT analysis, and the Pareto principle have been impacting organizations for decades. All of these concepts were created from different standpoints. Maslow's hierarchy of needs provides a psychological theory of human motivation. From an economic perspective, Schumpeter's concept of creative destruction focuses on innovation and productivity, while Pareto's 80/20 rule focuses on efficiency distribution to maximize outputs. Other theories, like the five dysfunctions of a team or the goals, roles, processes, and interpersonal relations (GRPI) model (Tartell 2016), have been used to improve teams' performance.

We can also use these theories and concepts to develop a structured way of thinking to apply to daily life and decisions. That structure is associated with clear ideas, identified scale of values and needs, prioritization, and informed decisions. It is also associated with simplifying the life equation and integrating faith in life as a fundamental factor.

There are countless aspects that surround change, and often, challenges arise in the execution. The root of the actions are the decisions, and in many cases, choice is surrounded by fear, loneliness, and uncertainty. The goal is to integrate concepts to develop a Life Management Approach as a tool to make better choices. More than just simple choices, our decisions lead us to a balanced and meaningful life.

The framework development requires self-analysis and deep inner thinking because it is a very personal exercise. Only when we are happy and at peace with ourselves can we bring happiness and peace to others. Integrating these concepts into real life demands a lot of self-discipline, but instead of viewing it as rigid, we should look at discipline as a great gift that we give to ourselves.

The LMA calls for focus on ourselves (and not on others). It requires that we concentrate on opportunities (even in adversity) and align the most important resources (time, energy, and money) with what really has value. Because in the end, it's your life, it's your business.

CHAPTER 2

CREATIVE DESTRUCTION

A s we begin developing our four pillars and endeavor to nurture more meaningful futures, we must start by reinventing. By applying small changes consistently over time, we can create something new.

The term "creative destruction" was developed by the economist and author Joseph Schumpeter in the 1940s. In his book *Capitalism, Socialism and Democracy*, he explores the role of entrepreneurs and innovation in society to drive economic progress (Schumpeter 1950). His theories on entrepreneurship's role in economic development is one of his major contributions. In his explanation of the entrepreneurial process, Schumpeter introduced new products and new services while destroying or displacing the old ones. He viewed entrepreneurs as more than business owners but rather as people that introduced new ideas, thus new products, services, and production methods. Schumpeter thought that the profit of a business was driven by the entrepreneur's ability to innovate.

Creative destruction basically refers to the transformation of traditional business and economic models into new processes, with the goal of improving the standards of living (Nevshehir 2021).

High level, it's a combination of technology development and a constant search for opportunities to improve the processes of a business, independent of the leadership position in the economy. This improvement will result in better productivity and a stronger competitive position. Schumpeter thought that innovation is not only invention; it is also improved technologies, improved finance, and enhanced organizations.

To achieve the results proposed in the creative-destruction process, restructuring and resource reallocation is required to liberate the resources needed for new models or investments. This restructuring process has winners and losers. It comes with the displacement of resources no longer needed in the innovative model. The concept of creative destruction—and the resource replacement on which it is predicated—can be seen in today's economy with the transformation of several models that directly impact our daily lives. An example of creative destruction is the internet. Started decades ago as a new communication protocol between computers, it has since evolved to what we know today as the virtual age. That technological revolution has delivered products and services that have changed modern society's way of living. These new trends transformed a lot of areas, from the education and healthcare sectors to the way we work and do business. In a lot of these cases, the new trend has displaced previous models. Here are some examples:

- Email as a communication tool has replaced the traditional paper letter that took days or weeks to get to recipients.
- Uber and Lyft have revolutionized transportation models, especially in big cities, changing the previous taxi/bus model.

- Netflix, Hulu, and other streaming services have transformed the previous movie-rental model.

- Platforms like Airbnb and Vrbo have changed the way people do vacations, adding new competitors to the hotel industry.

- Teladoc and other companies are changing healthcare models with telemedicine services, offering virtual visits to patients—mainly for checkups, urgent care, and mental health.

Another example a of revolutionary trend is social media, which emerged around 2000, connecting people within countries and revolutionizing previous marketing concepts and advertising practices. Also, terms we commonly hear these days, like metaverse and cryptocurrency, are here to disrupt the way we view the exchange of goods and current economic trends.

There are many arguments for and against the creative-destruction process. The topic goes deeper in economic theory with discussions about job relocation, technology transfer, productivity, economic models, and the impact on public policy. We are not going to expand in that direction in this chapter, but rather, we are going to focus on the aspects related to continuous improvement and reinvention.

Finding New Ways

The relevance of creative destruction in the LMA is focused on looking at new ways to do things. It is about having a mindset of innovation and growth, which helps the individual move to a better state on a personal or professional level. The value of the creative-destruction concept is related to the development of a human being's ability to create new things, use new resources, or reinvent themselves. There are two main points of creative destruction that can be adapted to our personal lives: **innovation** and **reengineering**.

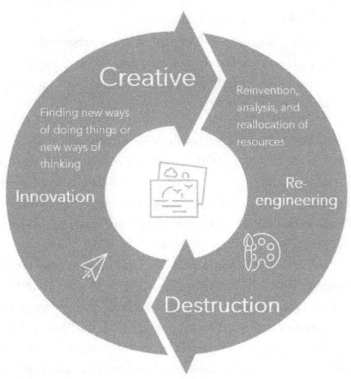

Innovation

The theory of creative destruction talks a lot about the value of innovation in the entrepreneurial process. Innovation could be a new product, but it could also be a new way of doing things, or even a new way of thinking. Finding new ways of doing things or new ways of thinking in our personal lives or careers is where the positive results are.

Constant learning is a key part of the personal and professional innovation process. Learning is not a "school age" concept. No matter your age, there are always benefits of learning that can make our lives better. That learning helps to create new paradigms, new life views, or new habits that bring improvements.

The best way to implement constant learning is by focusing on the strength and development of your four pillars. A good start could be dedicating time to reading and educating yourself on relevant topics that help to enrich your physical, emotional, spiritual, and financial health. One example could be reading twenty minutes a day, which would result in reading more than fifteen books a year, on average.

When I started my consulting company, I realized that I had strong business knowledge due to my educational background and corporate experience. But I recognized that there was a lot more I needed to learn about the overall consulting industry. To address that gap, I enrolled in a consultant's development program. I spent months learning about how to build an elite consulting business. I also read books (and listened to audiobooks) about consulting and coaching to expand my knowledge on how to create and manage a successful consulting company and to learn about what the winning consulting companies do versus the unsuccessful companies. I just tried to educate myself as much as possible on relevant topics to fulfill my current needs and my future plans.

The content we consume is fundamental to the learning and innovation framework because it must have a purpose. We can spend twenty minutes watching cat videos on social media, or we can spend twenty minutes reading or listening to an audiobook that helps us to expand our knowledge on a topic relevant to our current reality or future plans. The internet is a great tool, but it's also one of the main sources of distraction.

It is important to watch what we consume and control the time we spend on it.

One example of cutting the internet as a distraction is controlling the time spent on social media. The average American spends two hours per day on social media. Imagine what you could do with fourteen hours of personal learning per week—that's more than a full workday of development per week. There is nothing wrong with being connected with our friends and family or being aware of the latest fashion or business trends. The issue is when we spend unlimited time on these platforms with no purpose—time we could be using for other activities that lead us to our growth. Some apps have settings to control the time usage per day. The bottom line is that we should pay attention to the quantity and quality of the content we consume daily.

Another example of maximizing time and information is the news. Watching the news these days is a source of worry, demotivation, and negative energy. Too much polarization and bad news is out there. But it is good to be informed about things that can impact our life. Selecting a few city and community networks or news sources can keep you informed of things that could have direct relevance in your life. And if you want to be informed of other things, you can just search for them without being saturated by irrelevant information.

The learning framework is not knowledge just to know something. The value is in what I call **executable knowledge**: learning that helps us to make better decisions, develop better approaches, and face life in a better way. Ask yourself what you are getting from your time every day—what have you recently learned that helps you to improve your four main pillars or to better allocate your personal resources?

It is important to identify and make the time for that learning process. With our established routines, it could be easier just to say, "I don't have time for that." At the beginning, it is not easy, but once it is established, it becomes a very positive habit.

For example, when I had my baby—as any first-time parent knows—the baby did not come with an instruction manual. There were a lot of things we needed to learn. It was definitely a life-changing event for my husband and me. As a new mom, I decided it was good to learn "on the job" but also important to educate myself on the topic of parenthood. I understood that I had to learn more since it was a subject that would be part of my life for years to come.

In this case, I didn't enroll in any parenthood development program—there was no time for that. I was too tired and too busy in the first months of maternity to read paperback books, so I turned to audiobooks and short articles to start educating myself. Short periods of time spent consistently over a few years made a big difference. Integrating the constant learning was helpful to expand my perspective, manage my marriage as a new mom, keep my work–life balance in line, and develop a healthy daily routine. It was also helpful to integrate a framework of love, structure, and emotional balance in that new phase.

Building my company and how I managed maternity are two examples of finding new ways of doing things or a new way of thinking through a constant learning framework. I could have created my company with previous knowledge and lived the first years of maternity just learning "on the job." However, my view was that I wanted to do better. The same can be applied to your life. Yes, we can learn on the job, but constant learning will open doors to new perspectives, address the situation in a different way, and allow us to make more confident and informed decisions.

In summary, the innovation process is focused on the development of new paradigms, new life views, and new habits through constant learning. Look for specific areas of development in your life—it could be personal or professional. Once you identify the development areas, select the best learning resource for you. This could be formal or informal education. At this point, you have been creating a personal learning plan, and you should designate time to execute that plan. I recommend starting with short periods of time in a consistent way. And remember, the learning should be toward a goal and should be executable knowledge.

Reengineering

Destruction or disruption comes with opportunities. Whether it's easy, silly, or challenging—or sometimes painful—how we handle disruption or destruction can be the difference between winners and losers. Winners don't always win, but they see an opportunity to learn and improve in every loss. Losers sit on the bench to complain about failure, blame others, and go on about how unfair everything is.

The personal reengineering process is the analysis and reallocation of your resources to create change. This change could be an enhancement or the reinvention of the current state. We all have resources we use that are diverse and limited. The tools I have at this point in my life are not the same tools I had twenty years ago. Resources are the things you count on—it could be financial resources, skills and talents, your inner circle, your network, and your career experience. These resources should be aligned to your current needs and future plans. If you want to improve or create change with the same mindset, using the same resources, guess what the results will be? The chances of zero results are very high. Different results require different strategies, and the resources should be aligned to that new strategy.

The reengineering process is also associated with the ability to reinvent ourselves and transform a negative event into an opportunity. But this does not happen overnight. It requires focus and work to develop the mindset. It is that mindset that will lead to different actions and create change or different results.

Personal Creative Destruction

When I met Luciana and her fiancé, they were very happy working on their wedding plans. They decided they would pay for the party, honeymoon, and housing because they didn't want to be an economic burden for their parents.

Months before the wedding Luciana suddenly lost her job. She was sad about the event because she liked her job, she was delivering well, and she had no bad performance indicators or management observations. In the days after, she felt like she was in the middle of a storm. She was worried about the short-term plans of their wedding, but she was also worried about her professional future.

Luciana was not prepared for that adverse moment; she was confused and lost clarity about her professional future. Without income, all of her personal short-term plans were at risk. At that moment, she realized how much impact her job had on her personal life.

There were a lot of questions in her head. Would she find a new job soon? Should they cancel or postpone their personal plans? Ultimately, the reasons for why or what happened were not relevant anymore. The important question was: what was Luciana going to do with that adverse moment?

It was a wakeup call for her, and she took it as a learning opportunity that changed her view and career in a positive way. Luciana took time to think about the overall situation and how things didn't always go exactly as planned—and sometimes that was good. She and her fiancé decided to continue with their personal plans and keep the budget as low as possible.

Being laid off helped her to understand that while she'd had employment, she didn't have a mid and long-term plan for her career and her life. That was something she vaguely thought about years before but was not able to conceptualize or shape up. Losing her job led to doing the internal analysis that would help her to define a career plan for the next five to ten years. That plan consisted of a real integration of her career and her personal life, and it included having different roles or diverse experience. These aspects within a framework would lead to a simpler, balanced, healthy, drama-free, and happier life.

Luciana believed that marriage, family, and career went together. She felt that if these aspects were not aligned, the well-being of one of them could be at risk. She took the time to think, to conceptualize what she wanted and didn't want from her career, making sure that whatever she pursued was aligned with the other important variables of her life.

As with any business or project, execution is the hard part. The implementation of her personal and career plan was surrounded by difficult decisions. Luciana and her husband decided to relocate to a completely new place. She accepted jobs that required no previous experience, and she left behind friends and family. She made these moves without a guarantee of success, with only the goal to achieve better opportunities and the work–life balance she and her husband wanted.

Going through the hard part of execution was a wonderful reinvention and evolution process for Luciana. The negative event of being laid off helped her to create the path to who she is today. It was tough. It took time, but it was an eye-opener for her. She and her husband managed the unexpected together as a couple, and they prioritized and achieved their goal. She used creative destruction by planning for her long-term career (finding new ways of doing things), identifying what she wanted and didn't want, and allocating her resources toward what was important for her (family and career balance). What started as a stressful and overwhelming situation ended up being a great life lesson and a trigger for growth.

Winners and Losers

Creative destruction is not without pain. The theory refers to the job or employment aspect and the job loss that occurs as a result of a skills gap. Workers that cannot adapt to the new trends are left behind, while workers that can adapt will take advantage of the opportunity. In the creative-destruction theory, this is the result of a breach between the introduction of new practices and the sector that struggles to fit into the new model. According to the theory, this is common in workers that lack a formal education or skills that help them to align their talent to the new model or economy.

In the theory of creative destruction, there is inevitable displacement of resources no longer needed in the innovated or improved model. The new model could be a new process, new companies, or new industries. And in this new model, there are going to be resources that are going to be relegated. This is the unfriendly aspect to the theory. Unfortunately, we have seen how new trends and industries impact sectors of the workforce that didn't adapt (for whatever reason) to the new scenarios.

When we bring a theory into our personal lives, there are sometimes going to be winners and losers in the process. We should not intend to create change doing the same things we have been doing for years. Different results sometimes required different strategies. As part of the plan, it's important to evaluate the resources available and how those resources are aligned with our plans. For example, how do your time, money, and energy align with the new framework? Is your current network supporting future goals? You can say you want to spend more time with your family, and that your family is your priority, but does your schedule and agenda support that statement?

The personal creative-destruction process will require letting go of things, habits, and people that are no longer aligned or who are blocking our goals and improvement plans. On the other hand, this displacement will give way to bringing in new learning, practices, networks, and other resources that support future plans.

To improve my physical and mental pillars, I worked on my eating and sleeping habits. I educated myself about healthy eating, increased the number of fruits and veggies in my diet, cut sugars (such as cookies, cake, and ice cream), and eliminated fried and highly processed foods from my fridge and menus. It was not a sudden change, but small changes over time gave me the results I wanted. I shifted my mindset from putting the attention only on weight or clothing size to centering my attention on cleaner and healthier eating habits. Similarly, I adjusted my sleeping habits to have more energy and a more productive day. I adopted a rigid sleep schedule that allows me to sleep eight hours a night—I go to bed before 9:00 p.m. and wake up at 5:00 a.m. The changes helped me to feel energized and have more effective days.

One important element of daily productivity is ensuring you have a clear purpose for each day. What do you want to achieve today, or what do you need to get done today? Having a clear purpose helps to start your day with direction and be motivated to get things done. Like any other change in habits, it takes time and discipline, but it is worth it.

A *clear mind* is essential to focus on your goals and avoid distractions that would take you away from your plan. Distancing yourself from toxicity really helps. Sometimes there are people who bring a lot of negativity. In my case, to protect my energy as one valuable resource, I decided I needed to pay attention to that part of my life for my own progress and peace of mind. It was a multiyear effort to put the right distance between myself and the people who, at some point, were close and influential to me but who were bringing me negativity. This was the hardest part, but I can say that my walk is lighter and more meaningful now.

This is not an approach associated with throw-away mindset in which we use and dispose at out convenience. Nor does it refer to the idea of packing one bag and going to the Himalayas. This concept focuses on the results of slight changes applied over time in a consistent way. It's focused on the constant work with ourselves aimed at innovation, constant learning, creating, and seeking new opportunities in our careers and in our personal lives.

Personal creative destruction does not come overnight. It takes time and discipline. It can be triggered by a negative event like losing a job, a failed relationship, or a bad business. Or it can arise from a deep desire for a better life. Whatever the reason that motivates the change, these processes often come with fear, loneliness, and uncertainty. The focus on personal innovation centers on finding or learn new ways of doing things or new ways of thinking, while individual reengineering pursues the reallocation of resources to support that personal innovation. The overall reinvention process is intended to make us take the best of the worst, which makes the difference in life. That difference is made every day, with structure, a visualized plan, and small victories. That is what makes the contrast between destruction and creative destruction.

CHAPTER 3

NEEDS AND VALUES

Once we understand that a new way of thinking is necessary to create meaningful change in our lives, the natural question is how we can determine which thoughts we should prioritize to achieve that fuller life. When considering potential avenues for change, it is important to first identify the needs and values that form the core of who you are—or who you want to be. Once again, we can consult business and organizational development principles to help us navigate these challenges.

Maslow's hierarchy of needs is a theory of human motivation created by the psychologist Abraham Maslow (McLeod 2023). His study was focused on human needs and motivation and how the fulfillment of those needs was strongly correlated with individual happiness. Even though the theory was established eighty years ago, it still has a great influence on organizational development, management, and the overall business world of today. Organizations have been using the hierarchy of needs for years to support policies and practices that increase overall motivation and enable the workforce to reach higher levels of potential.

Maslow came up with a pyramid to express that people are motivated by five levels of needs: (1) physiological needs, (2) safety and security needs, (3) love and belonging needs, (4) esteem and prestige needs, and (5) self-actualization needs. Often, the pyramid is divided into three groups. The lowest levels of the pyramid contain the most basic needs, while the most complex needs are at the top. Basic needs include physiological requirements and safety. The next level comprises psychological needs like belonging and self-esteem. Finally, at the highest level, individuals can address their need for self-fulfillment. Others divide the five parts of the pyramid between material (physiological and safety) and psychological needs (belonging, esteem, and self-actualization).

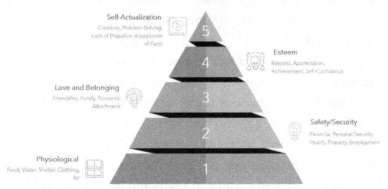

MASLOW'S HIERARCHY OF NEEDS

We can break down the five sections as follows:

- **Physiological:** The first level of the pyramid includes the basic needs critical for human living. Some examples are food, water, clothing, shelter, and sleep. At the organizational level, this could be a safe work environment, proper restrooms, access to water, break areas and time to eat meals, and clean facilities.

- **Safety:** This need refers to the sense of protection, order, and control that individuals want in life. It includes employment, access to health insurance, proper housing, and financial stability, such as contributing to savings and retirement accounts. In the workplace, this could be better ergonomics, such as proper lighting and furniture, as well as a sense of respect, safety, and job stability.

- **Love and Belonging:** This includes the emotional relationship and the connection to others. Personal relationships with family, couple relations, and friends are at the top of the list. Social, community, and religious groups are also part of the sense of connection included in this need. This part of the pyramid is addressed in a different way at the workplace, with a focus on creating an environment in which employees have a sense of belonging and feel that they fit within the company culture, mission, and individual teams. When this happens, it is easier for workers to feel motivated to be high performers, achieve business goals, and deliver better results.

- **Esteem:** At the fourth level of the pyramid, it becomes important to gain respect and appreciation from others. Recognition from others gives the individual a sense of confidence. Yes, this is a kind of ego need in the human environment to feel secure in our social groups, such as family circles, social entities, and work teams. In the workplace, this can be manifested through recognition for the achievement of results, a sense of growth, and positive feedback.

- **Self-Actualization:** At the top of the pyramid, the individual achieves a process of growing and developing their full potential. They focus on building their talents and maximizing their creativity with better problem-solving skills and eliminating prejudice, concentrating mainly on themselves and self-development. At the workplace, the employee feels that they can add input or give feedback to senior leadership and feel comfortable using their creativity and exploring their talents.

The Impact of the Pyramid

The hierarchy of needs, although used in business, is also very useful for personal life. The pyramid is a visual representation of a life lived in harmony and fulfillment. In that sense, it helps to conceptualize the importance of balance through prioritization. What is really important in our lives is what should drive actions; the rest is secondary. Those priorities should be tied to our scale of values and vision of the future. The hierarchy of needs is a useful tool for clearly defining how to satisfy each of our personal needs and how those needs are aligned with future goals.

This theory is not intended to create perfect enterprises or perfect employees. Neither is it intended to create a perfect life. It is just a tool to help us to organize our thoughts and establish real priorities. Life and the world are full of distractions, which makes it very easy for us to lose our North Star. Once we establish our needs and priorities, we can drive actions toward that North Star. In my case, I've integrated values such as family, love, empathy, continuous improvement, honesty, and transparency into my personal pyramid of needs.

When I was in my twenties, some close family members and friends made fun of me because I asked myself and asked them where they saw themselves in five to ten years. That question was in my subconscious and reflected in my quotidian conversations. It was part of a continuous inner process of self-analysis: *how do I visualize myself in the next decade?* It was not a step-by-step plan, but asking myself that question helped me to better visualize what I wanted and didn't want for my future.

Addressing Your Pyramid, Piece by Piece

Each quadrant in the pyramid can be filled with different items depending on our individual values and priorities. It is composed of a bunch of very personal decisions. For example, housing needs. We all have housing or shelter needs. Some people fill those needs by living with their parents; others rent city apartments, and some own a house in the suburbs. All address the same physiological need but in a different way. Analyzing the pyramid helps to identify how we want to fulfill each of these boxes in our lives.

Let's consider my friend Iris. Iris wanted to have her own financial resources and not be economically dependent in a relationship. She saw marriage as a path to walk together and build together with a partner, not as a dependency relationship. She identified under her safety and security quadrant that she wanted to have her own job, a retirement plan, and investments, and share with her partner the household responsibilities. On the other hand, she wanted to have time to be there for her family.

The visualization of all those things at the beginning looked inconsistent and overwhelming. But even though it looked difficult upon execution, Iris identified specific milestones to achieve her personal goals. In her case, like Luciana in the creative destruction, Iris identified the tools and resources needed to fulfill her safety and security quadrant. The decisions around those milestones were aligned to her career growth and relationship priorities. Iris created a multiyear plan with the conceptualization of her needs, based on her values.

Maslow's hierarchy was part of Iris's LMA. This thought structure helped to identify her core values, and then direct and prioritize the actions aligned to her values and needs. Those decisions allowed her to achieve the sense of security needed to move to the next level in the pyramid.

Once Iris felt that her physiological, safety, and love and belonging needs were fulfilled, that gave her the confidence to become a mom. She and her husband talked about parenthood as a great gift and responsibility, but they didn't feel ready to become parents until they defined their needs and worked on fulfilling them. After Iris worked on her personal pyramid of needs, she had more clarity about her life views and her priorities.

In her first year as a working mom, it was extremely challenging for Iris to keep her desired balance; sometimes she doubted it was realistic. But that balance was doable. All her previous decisions led to a lot of lessons to become a better version of herself. The personal exercise of establishing her needs led to honest conversations and plans that facilitated the decision-making process—or actions (which are what matter).

It was a beautiful and rewarding process that gave Iris the self-confidence to move to the next level. Once established as a working mom and comfortable as part of a married couple with children, Iris felt ready to start accelerating her career. Leaving a lot of fears behind, Iris now had a clear and enthusiastic vision of the future. She realized that without knowing it, she was already working in her self-actualization quadrant, meaning she was doing things she had wanted to do for years but hadn't felt ready or confident to do. Some good things about the self-actualization quadrant are the focus on creativity and the lack of prejudice. Focusing on individual values and needs helps to drop some emotional ballast and allows you to walk more lightly with what is meaningful.

Keeping a balance between the different quadrants is very important. Some people tend to focus more on only one or two needs or on material needs over spiritual needs and vice versa. The focus on only one need or a group of needs creates an imbalance in life. That is why it's important to keep all the quadrants in perspective and pay attention to all of them.

Also, it's important to be aware that it is not a tool for perfection but rather a way to create balance and harmony that will lead to a richer emotional life. Each of the needs are not always going to be 100 percent fulfilled to be ready to move to the next phase. And even when you get to the next phase or to self-actualization, you are not done. The pyramid requires constant revision as part of the framework for continuous improvement and a growth mindset.

One of the things I like about this theory is that rather than focusing on abnormal behaviors, Maslow's approach focuses on the development of healthy individuals. I identify with this approach because I believe that focusing on the positive aspects is fundamental for personal growth. Love, empathy, faith, and a growth mindset will lead us to a better path in life. The challenge is making those small decisions that will take us there.

The Pyramid and the Value Definition

The personal hierarchy of needs provides the structure to align personal values and needs with actions. Each quadrant or need can be fulfilled with a lot of different things. The scale of values helps to clearly define how to fill each of the quadrants based on our core values, and not with whatever is out there.

By taking the time to identify our core values, decision-making becomes clearer and more objective. Values are like the foundation of a house, providing the base for choices, actions, and behaviors. It helps us to make our own decisions and not make personal choices based on external influences like social media or what other people do. Core values are much more than a bunch of pretty words. They identify what is important, and the challenge is how you express those values in your daily life, in both the small things and your personal choices. For example, one core value could be your personal wellness, which combines many factors between mind, body, and personal environment.

In my life, I am committed to turning core values into action. On the mental and spiritual side, I am constantly consuming spiritual and personal development books, audiobooks, or podcasts, learning from people who have transcended adversity or, in my opinion, have had a meaningful life. Many of these people have high levels of emotional intelligence and a growth mindset—two essential factors for my own personal growth.

In my environment, I try to keep personal areas clean and decluttered. Of course, that doesn't happen magically. There is no way I can deliver my intended results if I am the only one taking care of the house. We have created a series of rules or systems for coexistence at home, making this a family habit we can only achieve through teamwork. My husband and I have made this happen through constant conversation and balancing and rebalancing our workload. Kids learn by observation, so watching Mom and Dad helping each other every day is the best lesson and a way to make kids part of the helping team. As with any habit, this doesn't happen overnight, and sometimes we do things we don't necessarily love to do (like cooking, in my case). But the focus should be on the end goal of family wellness.

As part of a focus on my environment, I watch the people that surround me. I agree with the theory that we are greatly influenced—whether we like it or not—by the people who are closest to us. That has been one of my most significant changes in the last few years. I now pay more attention to the quality of my relationships rather than the quantity. This has helped me to be more selective about who I spend my time with and what kind of energy I'm getting from the people that are closer to me.

Easier Said Than Done

Living by your core values is not as easy as saying it. It requires focus and emotional intelligence to act based on your convictions and not based on what others think. This doesn't mean you need to be selfish or live in a bubble; it's just that living your life on your terms is going to draw criticism and judgment.

Let's take my good friend Nanny as an example. Two of Nanny's core values are honesty and transparency. For her, lies and hypocrisy are like a weed that silently damages relationships over time. She saw how in the past, close relationships were broken just because she was honest and transparent. In those moments, it was very difficult because she felt confused, thinking maybe she was wrong or that she had been selfish or careless. But with the passing of time, through self-analysis of personal needs and values, Nanny realized that she did the right thing because she acted according to her values. If she had done things in a different way, she would have strayed from her values and acted according to other people's terms.

Example of Core Values

learning care
gratitude balance learning wellness
prosperity
integrity love family honesty
freedom happiness
faith respect
compassion
generosity

There is a strong interrelationship between the exercise of identifying core values and the hierarchy of needs. The combination consists of the pyramid—intended to identify your needs—and the core values, which help to answer how you are going to fulfill your needs based on your best interests.

The importance relies on focus, thought structure, and a better vision of life and the future to act toward a plan. Having a strong view of your core values and integrating them with the pyramid provides more clarity and objectivity to make small and big decisions. Using this approach also helps manage conflicts by reminding us of what is important and helping us to avoid the drama. When you are clear about your priorities, you don't get distracted by small things, and that helps you move forward.

Core Elements to Drive Actions

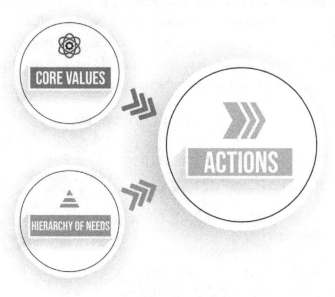

Applying these concepts to your personal life can be as easy or as complex as you want to make it. As with any change management plan, it takes time, discipline, and constant revision. Of course, there are some scenarios that are more challenging than others. But those tough scenarios will change you more for the good if you embrace them. Your approach can make all the difference between whether it works or not. Some people may think that the Life Management Approach is not for them—and maybe it's not for everyone. The value is when you see it as a development tool, as something that will help you to manage the small things.

There are a lot of distractions in life that can add so much useless noise to your mind and soul. The hierarchy of needs and defining your core values is just a way to organize your thoughts, to prioritize, to take out what's not adding value, and to keep the things that really have value. Once you define these aspects, you will be in better shape to take action. That readiness results in more confidence and making decisions based on what matters to you. At that moment, you will feel that you are simplifying your life equation and that you're ready for the next level.

CHAPTER 4

SWOT

Identifying your needs and values helps provide direction for your life. In order to capitalize on the opportunities to successfully integrate those needs and values, however, it's crucial that you are able to objectively assess your own strengths and weaknesses. There is another business concept you can add to your toolbox for success.

The SWOT analysis is a method commonly used in business schools and applied in organizations. It focuses on the analysis of a company's strengths, weaknesses, opportunities, and threats. The assessment provides valuable input for decision-making and strategic or business development plans. It is very common to see the SWOT in marketing, but it's also useful and valuable in other areas.

The model captures internal and external factors of the business and divides it into positive and negative aspects. Internal factors are the strengths and weaknesses—things with a high chance of internal control. External variables are the opportunities and threats. Since these are outside of the organization, they cannot be controlled. However, even if there is no direct control, it doesn't mean they should be ignored; these factors may still be addressed, mitigated, or maximized. As part of the strategic planning process, companies also analyze internal and external scenarios to examine the company's current competitive position and design future strategies that allow them to hold or increase their position in the market.

In the same way that organizations have strengths, weaknesses, opportunities, and threats, we as individuals also have our SWOT. Even if the answers look very different from a corporate SWOT, the main goal is the same: to create awareness of important factors that impact our decision-making or personal strategy.

As an individual, the personal SWOT should have an objective, and we should be honest about the answers if we want to use it as a decision-making tool. The SWOT is not just for fun (unless we're really bored). It's a tool that helps us make choices or bring clarity throughout the decision-making process. The analysis should have a purpose and have a clear route to action.

A personal SWOT is a self-evaluation tool that facilitates an assessment when it comes to career growth, self-development, and management of change. It's more than a fancy management tool used by consultants. It helps you get a picture of your current situation in a simple visual way. Unlike the pyramid of needs, the SWOT doesn't have a hierarchy; it's usually arranged in a quadrant without order of importance. The assessment is not about filling in the blanks. The value of the exercise is in the actions that follow the analysis. Let's look at the different factors.

Strengths

Strengths are the internal positive aspects or things you can control. In business, for example, the S quadrant tries to answer questions like "What are your competitive advantages?" or "What resources are available?" In your personal life, this could be your skills, education, and experience.

Weaknesses

For a company, weaknesses are internal negative attributes that can sometimes overshadow its strengths. For example, the W tries to answer the question "Where can we improve?" Individuals can likely find things to improve as well. Also, there might be things you're not comfortable with but that you have some level of control over.

Opportunities

Opportunities are positive factors that can benefit or potentially help the success of a business. The O attempts to answer questions like "In what segments can we try to increase sales or market share?" In personal life, opportunities could be a new job market trend you can take advantage of or new business opportunities. This quadrant is very broad, so it is important to work internally to identify and take advantage of the opportunities.

Threats

Threats are the negative external variables that you have no control over and that can screw up your plans. Even if you don't have direct control, though, there are actions you can take to navigate, avoid, or minimize threats. In business, the **T** quadrant tries to answer questions like "What environmental factors (such as regulations and market trends) are threatening the company or the product?" Identifying your personal threats is important too because it creates awareness about your vulnerabilities. For example, being aware of job market trends and your personal position toward them could help you identify options to reduce individual risk in an adverse turn.

Example of a Personal SWOT

INTERNAL FACTORS	EXTERNAL FACTORS
STRENGTHS	**OPPORTUNITIES**
-Skills -Education -Personal resources -Achievements	-New job market trends -Business startup -Business development
WEAKNESSES	**THREATS**
-Areas you're uncomfortable with -Low emotional intelligence -Financial disorganization -Bad habits	-Decrease in job market demands -Industry changes -Competition

POSITIVE

NEGATIVE

THE PERSONAL SWOT

SWOT on Your Decisions

When I met Vickie, she was finishing college and had started thinking about a career change. She had a full-time job at a good company, but she thought her current job wouldn't take her to the level she aspired to in her career. Her job satisfaction was pretty good, so she felt there wasn't a solid reason for a change. She liked what she was doing, had a good boss, and was comfortable with her execution. On the other hand, she knew she could have a better salary, and she was concerned about the idea of seeing herself twenty years later in the same chair, doing exactly the same thing. She knew it was time to start working on her long-term career plans, but she wasn't sure where to start or what to change.

As part of her role, she worked closely with executives. One day, she was getting out of a meeting and had a chat with one of the executives. She asked Vickie if she ever considered moving to another area of the business. Her immediate answer was no. A career change was just a thought. She hadn't shared that with anyone. During the chat, the executive told her that she should consider a job change because she had a lot of skills that could be maximized and developed in other areas of the business. Also, other roles would offer better salaries and opportunities. "And of course," the executive said, "don't tell your boss I told you that."

That was Vickie's "aha" moment—or her SWOT moment. She realized it was time to start actively working toward a career change. She felt that she needed to take action, so she sat down and worked on the exercise, analyzing her strengths, weaknesses, opportunities, and threats. For example, she realized that even though she considered herself shy, she was good at working with teams and managing difficult people and conversations, and she was strongly solutions-oriented. Once she identified her **strengths,** she realized she had control over how to maximize them in her favor during the career-movement process. By clearly knowing what our strengths are, we have a greater chance of selling those skills and making the most of them in our favor. Assessments like the Myers–Briggs Type Indicator (MBTI) can also help identify our strengths.

As part of the self-evaluation process, Vickie acknowledged that her technical skills were one of her **weaknesses**. She identified that as something she needed to work on and strengthen if she wanted to grow in the business. The current job market was a **threat** for her, with a saturated labor market and overall deteriorated economic indicators in her area. She had no control of the current economic environment. However, she identified a possible **opportunity**: she could remain with her current employer but relocate to another city with a stronger job market and better economic outlook.

Working on her SWOT helped give Vickie the clarity to move forward in her next steps—a career change. But after answering all the questions, she was scared because to move forward with a plan, she would have to make big changes in her life. The actions would completely take her out of her comfort zone, and at times, there would be more questions than answers. But she bet on herself and allocated her main resources (time, money, and energy) on that short-term change with an expectation of better long-term results.

Vickie's plans were not well received by her personal and professional circle. Some of her peers told her that they just didn't understand her move if she was fine where she was. Overall, it was an overflow of opinions and advice ranging from "You don't know what you want" to "That's not going to work." Vickie was making an unpopular decision to achieve what she thought was best for her future.

At the beginning, it was tough for her. Initially, she didn't get the salary increase she was expecting, and she accepted jobs she didn't enjoy. Some days, Vickie doubted she made the right decision. She felt out of place, and sometimes she felt she had failed. But her gut told her to keep walking and stay focused. And that's what she did. Her patience and perseverance helped her get to where she wanted to be. Later, she understood that the uncomfortable period she'd gone through was part of the learning process. Sometimes, feeling uncomfortable or challenged is good for development because the resistance helps us not to quit. The personal SWOT was the foundation for Vickie's execution. It gave her clarity for a career-development plan. It was still her responsibility to take action, but the personal SWOT provided the groundwork.

Put SWOT to Work for You

A common question might be "What should I do with each quadrant?" Since there are internal and external factors, it's good to separate them based on the level of control and impact. The internal factors are things you have direct control over but that you will not necessarily be able to change. The weaknesses can be improved and developed without turning them into strengths.

For example, when I was in high school, I was one of the worst in my class at math. I avoided math-related classes in college as much as possible. I was not open to learning and used the excuse that I "just wasn't good at it." I now think that was a kind of mental laziness. It was easier to use that excuse rather than put myself to work to improve. But that rejection and running away from my "weakness" was limiting my development opportunities. Not addressing my weakness was costing me. So, if I wanted to grow in my industry or gain strong business knowledge, I needed to improve my analytical skills.

There were no more reasons or justifications to avoid the numbers in my career plan. As an engineer and math lover, my husband helped me a lot to understand the value of the numbers integrated into a career. I started to see that weakness as an opportunity to improve. It's not that I suddenly loved math, but I was now mentally open to learning through training and exposure. That weakness did not become the strength. I may not have gained the know-how of a data scientist or a finance executive, but my analytical skills are significantly better. Addressing that weakness allowed me to successfully manage financial and strategic-planning data and to successfully lead business conversations.

Looking at the external variables, the **threats** are aspects we cannot change but that we can address. We can navigate the threats and be clear about whether we must make a decision. In Vickie's case, she couldn't control the job market; however, she took advantage of jobs or business opportunities outside of a specific location. The weaknesses and threats should not be seen as totally negative aspects. They're just part of the imperfect world in which we live. They're important because even if we can't control them, they help us to identify our vulnerabilities.

The **opportunities** are external factors over which there is no direct control but that you can take advantage of. You must look for them and identify them. Opportunities are out there; you have to pursue them, sometimes unceasingly. Opportunities are often time sensitive, which makes the decision-making process more challenging.

A lot of times, when an opportunity arrives, fear automatically arrives too. We want the perfect opportunity at the right time, and that is very rare. When Vickie got the opportunity to relocate to another city, she immediately received questions like "Why now? Can't you just wait for the next opportunity?" It could be that a better opportunity would've come along if she had waited—but you never know. Choices are usually risky, which is why it's important to decide based on the information you have at that moment.

Similar to the hierarchy of needs, the SWOT is a tool for self-evaluation. The pyramid is more focused on values and needs, while the SWOT is more oriented to a career and development plan. Both models can contribute to the development of a thought structure valuable to the decision-making process. It's not a perfect recipe and it will not tell you what to do. It just facilitates a way to make organized and clear decisions. It requires time to implement a clear idea and honesty to identify weaknesses and threats.

Sometimes, it can be useful to have feedback from mentors and others close to you. Always keep in mind that this is your exercise and not others'. It is preferable to keep it simple and have a clear understanding of why you are doing a personal SWOT. This is a tool to facilitate decision-making through organized ideas.

The SWOT (like the pyramid) isn't just an assessment or a process of thoughts and actions. We don't say, "Here are the diagrams. That's it." We should see it from an actionable standpoint like, "Here are the results of my assessment. Now let's make the results more relevant to my reality and my goals." This should also be a dynamic process. Your SWOT today might be different from your SWOT ten years ago, and that's good because it means you are moving on in your life and career. Skills development and learning new things is a never-ending exercise.

We should be constantly looking at how we can develop and maximize opportunities, manage weaknesses, and address threats. It is important to keep in mind that there is no right or wrong answer for this exercise. The answers are not absolute, and there are chances to change or address them. And at the root of this exercise is the objective to simplify your life, so keep the answers as simple as possible.

CHAPTER 5

80/20

As you continue to grow your toolbox of skills, you may feel more empowered to act on opportunities as they present themselves. Unfortunately, though, it's not always easy to decide which opportunities are worth pursuing and which are better left on the shelf. One way to elevate your decision-making process is to reflect on your priorities and consider how you can allocate your resources in a way that matches those priorities. Luckily, there is another business principle you can adopt to assist you in this process.

The 80/20 rule is also known as the Pareto principle and states that 80 percent of the results come from 20 percent of the actions. This principle was first introduced by an Italian philosopher and economist named Vilfredo Pareto in the first half of 1900. His research was more focused on the distribution of wealth in Italy, but his concept was later integrated into production, quality control, and many other business and strategic management areas.

Some examples of the Pareto principle in the business world are that 20 percent of the sales team make 80 percent of total sales, or 20 percent of customers generate 80 percent of total profits.

Organizations use this 80/20 rule to focus on the 20 percent of factors that will produce the best results. This doesn't mean that the other 80 percent should be ignored—it's a matter of **prioritization**. In these cases, the company should prioritize keeping the 20 percent segment maximized.

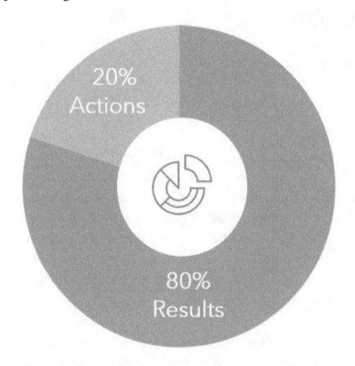

The core of the 80/20 concept is related to the distribution of resources and focuses on the core factors that maximize productivity. On the personal side, this 80/20 approach is very useful in decision-making, efficiency, and time management. In previous chapters, the integration of Maslow's hierarchy explained the importance of identifying our needs and values as part of the process to achieve balance. Meanwhile, the SWOT looked more into career, development, and growth. In this chapter, we'll see the integration of the Pareto principle in personal life through prioritization and distribution of resources. Prioritization and allocation of resources will help us to simplify our lives and make clearer and more thoughtful decisions.

Using Pareto to Establish Priorities

In my role as a project manager, I always tell the teams that if everything is a priority, then there are no priorities. In brainstorming meetings, it was common to see people explaining the criticality of xyz or insisting that if we change or replace a process that has been there for years, it would be the end of the company. It's a natural reaction to not let go at first. Understanding this natural reaction helps to manage the often difficult conversation about trade-offs and letting things go as part of the improvement process. The change management and prioritization process can be compared with the sales process. It is common to get pushback and resistance at the beginning, but good sales professionals master how to manage objections. Objections are a natural part of the sales process. It's important to address the objections with active listening and respect.

The prioritization process in organizations and business is like selling what we think is the best product or what is in the best interest of your customer. The prioritization process in life is very similar. But this time, the focus (and the 20 percent) is on what will help you maximize the results. In this case, you are your customer, and you must manage your own objections. Your own objections could be "I don't know" or "I can't" or "That's not for me." Or all the excuses that come to mind when we think about getting out of our comfort zone.

Identifying common objections is helpful to opening our minds and determining what really has value for us. As part of the process, we don't have to get too technical on the 20 percent versus the 80 percent. It's just a matter of assigning an order of importance to the things that really have value to our current lives and goals and distributing the resources accordingly. But that 20 percent should be specific and clear, and that can be challenging. It is a lot easier to tell others in a project what the best prioritization path is. In our personal life, it might take time to manage our objections. In some cases, it can be painful to accept that things are no longer aligned with our views and that we must let go.

The prioritization process could be by selection, by elimination, or both. The process flows better when it's aligned to our needs, values, and aspirations (development and growth). Having that in mind facilitates the drill-down to identify what the real priorities are (prioritization by selection) or what is really important to our current scenario, goals, and plans.

For example, a good way to identify individual priorities is to look at the four main pillars of well-being: physical, spiritual, mental, and financial. In my case, these four pillars are strictly aligned to my core values of faith, family, continuous development, and contribution. This facilitates my decision-making and the alignment of my 20 percent. Developing a thought process toward the 20 percent also allows us to separate between what is value-added and non-value-added. That assignment of value helps make it easier to say no without regrets.

We can also approach prioritization through a process of elimination. We can eliminate things that may have been good and important at some point—and that are not necessarily bad or harmful—but are no longer aligned to the core of our current needs and future plans. Assigning a lower level is not throwing it out completely; it's just assigning a weight to our priorities. The more open we are to letting go, the easier the process will be.

"That may sound easy, but it's not," you might say. Yes, sometimes it will be very difficult. That's when we must focus on what we really want, handle our own objections, and keep the excuses out of the game. Prioritization is not an easy process. If it were, everyone would have a balanced life. Once we establish our priorities, it's time to move to the distribution of resources.

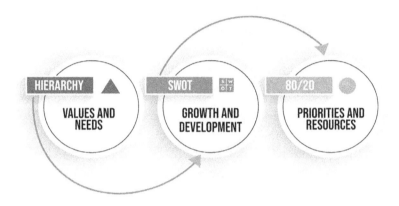

Time to Share

Prioritization is fundamental to achieving personal goals, and the prioritization process requires us to let things out. Far from displacing or disparaging some things in life, it's a process of assigning an order to what matters the most. Yes, you will have to let things go, and sometimes that's painful.

For my friends Xavi and Claire, sharing was one of their core family values. For their Christmas vacations, they decided they wanted to share with someone in need in the place they were traveling. The family vacation schedule was complete, and the plan was that they would visit a convent in a small town near their vacation spot. But there was a last-minute conflict with the planned "day of doing good," and the only chance to go was the day after

Christmas, which was when they had scheduled a beach day. There was already a boat rental, clear water, sun, and an opportunity to relax and enjoy good company on that day. Of course, they wanted to go to the beach, but they also wanted to take a pause in their busy corporate lives to connect with other people's needs.

When they talked about what they should do, they agreed what they didn't want was to get back home and say, "Oh, we were going to have a day of doing good, but there was no time." That would have been very uncomfortable for them because they wanted to have a family activity to show the little ones the value of sharing. To cancel the beach day, however, would be costly, and they could always plan another day of doing good when they got home. So, they asked themselves what they wanted to do with their time and what the priority was.

Those questions helped them to decide, and they changed the plan and went to the convent. That would be an unpopular decision for some, but it was the most rewarding for them. The convent was a humble and peaceful place. They walked with some of the younger nuns and visited some old or sick nuns who were bedridden. Even with all the challenges surrounding them, there was joy in that place. Claire and Xavi saw how others embraced their needs and challenges with a good spirit and in a positive way. They also saw how much people could do with limited resources, without complaint.

That visit reminded them of the fragility and vulnerability of life. It also showed them how faith can change the way to embrace life and manage adversity. When they returned home and talked about the visit, they felt confident they had allocated their important resources (time, energy, and money) to things that added the most value for them.

Prioritization is not the easiest part of the LMA. It's more focused on decisions aligned with our values and needs. In the case of Xavi and Claire, there were several options to choose from. However, they decided to simplify the equation and allocate their time to what had more weight for them, which was the family value of contribution.

Resources

Companies have limited resources, which they must balance and distribute wisely to operate and achieve their goals. These can be financial resources (such as cash, investments, or loans), human resources, physical resources (such as materials, equipment, or real estate), and intangible or intellectual resources (such as patents or copyrights). The distribution of resources doesn't depend on just one or two aspects. It can be a very complex equation made up of multiple variables such as market fluctuations, supplier availability, quarterly revenues, customer satisfaction, and time to deliver, among others. Added to this are last-minute problems such as quality issues, supplier decommits, last-minute deals, and natural disasters impacting the operations. The assignment of priorities is fundamental to successfully navigating a challenging business environment.

Resource allocation is a dynamic process—sometimes we are assertive, and other times we make mistakes. There will be successes and fiascos; there will be people who are happy with decisions and others who are unhappy. The key to prioritization is to exercise judgment and make choices in the best interest of the business, within an ethical framework, and with the information available at that moment. It is exactly the same process in your personal life: prioritize using judgment to make decisions in your best interest, within your values/needs framework, and with the information available at that moment.

Similar to business, in our personal life, we should actively distribute and allocate our resources (time, energy, and money) in alignment with our priorities, goals and needs. Are we spending our energy looking at other people's lives, with continued emotional battles among family and coworkers? Or are we putting our energy toward continuous improvement, plans, and growth? Are you spending your time watching TV, engaging in unconstructive or unhealthy relationships, or just living your days with a lazy Sunday mentality? Or are you aggressively looking at how you spend your days and what you are going to accomplish today, this week, this month, and beyond? Are you truly making time in your agenda for your goals and needs? Are you spending money just to impress others or on useless stuff? Or are you investing in the things that really have value for you and your growth?

These questions helped me turn off the TV, let go of a few people, remove negative energy and focuses positive insights, and change my consumption behavior. It was all part of my prioritization and 20 percent alignment process.

The Big Impact of the Daily Routine

Each day is a small piece of the puzzle of your life. It's a cumulative result of hours, days, and years. Of course, there are things out of our control, but what we become is largely a consequence of the small choices we make every day. Under this premise, time is one of the most valuable resources because it does not return. I think that's why over the years I have become obsessed with time management, punctuality, and quality time. At a certain point, I declared a war on laziness and time-wasting, and I started respecting my time and others' time more each day. I need to recognize that I am still working on my intolerance with unpunctual people, and I'm trying to work on it with a dose of empathy.

Time is a limited resource, but some people manage it as an endless resource. Others understand the value of time too far down the road, when there is no more time. Internalizing the value of time, I started to ask myself how that value is reflected in my actions. That's when I started micromanaging my days. As part of a time management effort, my husband and I defined a structure for our household activities, managing routines with discipline and always trying to stick to it.

For example, I always try to sleep eight hours a night and start my day around 5:00 a.m. with a shower, a glass of water, coffee, and silence before 6:00 a.m. I try to complete the most important task of the day before 10:00 a.m. as part of my priority distribution. I complete important consulting and coaching tasks, reading, and writing before 7:00 a.m., and I do my best to be on time for business calls and maximize meeting time, always keeping the main takeaways from each in mind.

Procrastination will always be lurking, which is why it is important to keep a schedule and try to avoid the "I'll do this later" mentality. Family activities at the beginning and end of the day are important for the family culture, and this requires quality time. In the morning, it's breakfast, school, etc. For me, it's important to make a real connection with my loved ones before we start with our daily responsibilities. At the end of the day, we stick to a routine of having dinner together at the table, after-dinner sharing, and house tasks. Of course, there are hectic mornings and evenings, but having a daily schedule helps us keep the alignment as a family and as individuals.

Some of these ideas might sound super basic, and I'm not saying that waking up at 5:00 a.m. or being on time for meetings will change your life. These are just examples of small things and simple ways to manage time and energy as part of an overall mindset.

With discipline and honest communication, this is possible. The value of a daily routine can be seen in the long term. Zoom out on your day to identify the value-added versus non-value-added activities. Start creating a daily schedule with valuable outputs in mind.

We should ask ourselves how our actions are supporting our priorities and how our schedules are reflecting those priorities. For example, as I mentioned before, if you say your family is first, ask yourself if your resource distribution (time, energy, and money) is supporting those priorities. If there is no time in your agenda to spend quality time with your family, then you have two choices: modify your schedule, or be honest with yourself and accept that you have other priorities.

If you want to accelerate your career, is working toward that goal included in your agenda? This may be a tough question because the answer could challenge the status quo. However, it is a way to measure and translate thoughts into actions. That is why the prioritization and resource-allocation process takes time and requires a lot of honesty and character.

The Many Hats

When my acquaintance Joan was in grad school, there was a period in which she wore multiple hats. She was doing her PhD thesis, had a full-time job, worked as a part-time university professor, and was recently married. She was very committed to professional development and her personal roles. People asked her how she managed all those hats at the same time. Applying the 80/20 principle on a micro level helped her to fulfill the roles by managing daily activities. She was focused on the 20 percent portion of each role, and that helped her to make better day-to-day time management decisions. To do this, she learned to say "No" or

"I can't," independent of the pressure or jokes that she was boring or antisocial.

Even using the 80/20 rule, at some point, Joan needed to pause and reevaluate her strategy at a macro level. It was working well from a time management standpoint, but she felt it wasn't 100 percent aligned with the four pillars. Her days were very long, and she felt that she needed to add more personal time to her schedule.

As part of the self-analysis and prioritization exercise, she reevaluated her 20 percent based on her current scenario and future career plans. Joan decided to only stay with the full-time job, finish her degree, and not pursue more college professor opportunities. She recognized that working as a part-time professor was secondary on her priority list at that time, and it was taking more time than initially expected.

It wasn't an easy decision because that was a great opportunity for any grad student. But it was time to take action and align the resources available to her needs, values, and future plans. Her decision included giving up some things to obtain the balance she was looking for. She gave up extra income, experience, and exposure at that moment. But having more personal time was worth it.

The reevaluation of resources helped her make a decision, and it was not an easy choice. She had to make financial adjustments because the change meant one less income, but she also maximized the resources of time and energy. This was a good exercise of prioritization, applying the idea that if there are a lot of priorities, then there are no priorities. In this case, Joan used the Life Management Approach to evaluate her current scenario versus her future plans and resources available. The exercise provoked change, and yes, it was difficult, but it was for the best.

We all have good and bad days, and at the beginning, the changes and new habits might be exhausting. But it is not all that different from other goal-seeking efforts. What you do today creates your future. Prioritization by selection or elimination can be achieved through small and consistent choices based on your values and needs. Pursuing a better version of yourself is possible through small and consistent actions because small choices lead to great rewards.

As we saw in the case of Xavi and Claire and in Joan's situation, an 80/20 approach is related to prioritization and resource distribution. The approach is highly focused on assigning an order of importance to things that are key for our well-being and future plans. It's also about working on the individual exercise of separating what is value-added versus non-value-added. The concept of 20 percent is helpful for putting things into perspective and placing them in a value-added "bucket." This helps us align resources with priorities, goals, and needs. In practice, for example, it could be related to time management as part of the personal operations model. In the end, we should support all the internal analysis and prioritization with actions—then, our habits and schedules will reflect our real priorities.

CHAPTER 6

SIMPLIFY THE EQUATION

When I was in high school, I failed algebra several times. It's not something I'm proud of, but looking at it now through adult eyes, I see that math was not the problem. It's not that I wasn't smart or that I lacked extrinsic motivation. It was a matter of focus—and maturity, of course. In addition to my parents, who had to pay for extra classes, the only one affected by my actions (or lack of action) was me. It didn't matter how much my parents or friends wanted to help me. I was the one who had to pay attention, practice, and take the tests—I was the one who had to take action.

Maybe the best lesson I learned from my high school algebra years was that life can be like a math equation. It can become so complex that no one can solve it. Or it can become null, taking us nowhere, with zero results. Within the equation, there are variables we can control and others that we cannot. We must assign more weight or importance to some variables, and we'll have to cancel or take out some others. It's up to each of us to manage and simplify our life equation. It may seem silly and unrealistic, but it is possible, and it's as simple or complex as we want it to be. In the end, you are the one who must commit to paying attention, practicing, and taking the test.

Simplifying Our Life Equation

Our life equation is made up of countless factors that occupy our minds daily—family, house, bills, health, job, and school, among others. Not to mention the culture of negativity out there in the media and on social platforms. All these factors, in addition to the large amount of information we access daily, can create a spiderweb in our minds, diverting our attention and making it difficult to make decisions. There is a massive amount of information that can distract us or simply demotivate us. Simplifying the equation requires eliminating or reducing the factors that steal—or attempt to steal—our most valuable resources. It is useful at the decision-making point, and like the other approaches, it helps to drill down and contemplate what is really important for our well-being.

Without being too detailed, the desired outcome should be clear and specific. For example, "I want to be better" is not clear and specific. It will not lead to action. Instead of "I want to be better," a more specific statement would be "I want to be more fit" or "I want to improve my finances" or "I want to strengthen my marriage." That will take you to the next level in the equation, such as "I want to be more fit by losing weight, reducing my cholesterol, or giving up cigarettes." If the desired outcome is to improve your financial situation, a clearer statement would be "I want to increase my income" or "I want to improve my savings or start investing." Once the desired outcome is clear and specific, then we can move to a more detailed "how to" process, which will help on the action or habit development.

In addition to the desired outcome, considering the values and needs discussed in previous chapters will be helpful in the drill-down thought process. Having a clear visualization or goal will help to move to the next phase in the equation, which is assigning weight to the different factors. In the weight-assignment process, we give a level of importance or weight to each variable. The importance is tied to the relevance of those factors in our life or our decisions. There are some factors that are easy to assign a high, positive value to, such as supportive relationships. But the weight could be either positive or negative, depending on the relationship. For example, a close relationship will have a high weight because it is close to you. If you have a toxic romantic relationship, that would be a high-weight, negative-value variable.

Once you have assigned a value to each factor, it is time to start canceling factors or reassigning values. In this phase, you work on canceling the variables that will not take you to a desired result or that are screwing up your equation. This phase requires a lot of honesty with yourself, and the execution sometimes requires you to take the bitter pill. Changing a habit, looking for another job, reducing negative interaction, and changing your environment are just a few examples commonly seen in the cancellation process at a macro level.

You can take the same approach for a one-time decision. What do you want or need? What are the things that really have value and a positive impact? What are the roadblocks or things that aren't helping you get to your desired outcome and move toward action? Keep in mind that the results of simplification aren't necessarily evident in the short term. That's why, in the practice of life management, we should consistently "keep it simple."

SIMPLIFY THE EQUATION

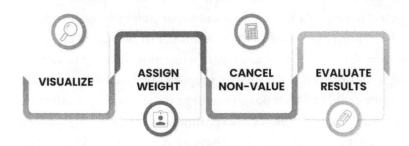

This keep-it-simple approach starts with the small things and extends to many other aspects in life. Like the pyramid, SWOT, 80/20, or any other life management method shared in previous chapters, the "simplify the equation" approach is not a sudden change. It takes time and effort to internalize it and take action.

Simple does not mean cheap, small, or insignificant. Simplicity is similar to the 20 percent approach, but in this case, it is tied to liberating and keeping clear the value added, or what is meaningful. Implementing this approach in different areas can drive extraordinary results. Simplification can start with the pillars of well-being (physical, spiritual, emotional, and financial) and the life equation through small things, and then extend to other important aspects of life. For example, in the physical part, I applied the simplification process to my eating habits. As I mentioned in a previous chapter, I integrated simple meal prep by reducing processed foods, fried foods, or high-sugar products. Changing my eating habits helped me to get more energy, stay at my desired weight, and not worry about the scale.

My business partner Jordan decided to start implementing the keep-it-simple approach in her consumption habits and in her environment. Having her workspace and her house in order has had a positive impact on her mood. Cleared, open, and decluttered spaces help with the flow of ideas and create an environment of order. Jordan believes personal physical spaces like houses and cars are a reflection of people's minds. Keeping our minds clean and decluttered helps us focus. She also implemented the approach of trying to keep her mind free of junk information, empty entertainment, or any kind of trashy content by filtering the information that she accesses daily.

Simplify Your Relationships

Another point to highlight under the keep-it-simple approach is the value of relationships. We are greatly influenced by the people we hang out with, especially our inner circle. Something as basic as everyday conversations have a great influence on our way of thinking. For example, if conversations with your partner always involve gossip about other people, endless criticism, how miserable or unlucky he or she is, or all kinds of toxicity, what do you think you'll have on your mind?

If you're already working on a more positive approach, you may feel mentally and emotionally disconnected from the person with whom you spend the most time. If that's the case, it's not that you should just get rid of your partner. Instead, it could be an area to work on together, if the goal is to move to a better mental state. Hypocrisy, envy, lies, a passive-aggressive attitude, and "friendly" bullying are factors that harm relationships and cause damage over time. Ignoring these signals because that person is nice or has some kind of tie with you can take your equation to a null or negative state; it can deplete your valuable resources (such as your time and energy).

This doesn't mean we should expect everyone to think or behave like us. Diversity of thought and opinions can help with personal enrichment. But a lot of the time, we know the crows who surround us. And if you don't know, pay attention to your feelings when you are around people. The energy and how you feel toward certain attitudes, treatment, or conversations will shed a little light for you.

Refusing to share your time and energy with toxic people, especially in your inner circle, is crucial to keeping it simple. It's not getting these people out of our lives. The key is to reduce and control the interaction and their level of influence on you. And no, we will not end up alone if we do this, because our focus will instead be on value-added relationships. We reduce the time and energy with the non-value-added relationship and focus on keeping and cultivating the value-added relationships. I decided to apply this approach because I realized that by not doing it, I was paying a high price with my time and energy for non-edifying and unconstructive relationships.

The reduction of time and influence doesn't happen overnight. I'm not going to call a "frenemy" and tell him or her, "Hey, you are not adding value for my life views. Please don't call anymore." The process of simplification is done with empathy and kindness, using time and space as a good tool. We don't want anyone to feel rejected or discarded, but the reality is that, with toxic people, sometimes there is no way to win. The focus should be on quality over quantity, similar to the 80/20 method.

This keep-it-simple approach applies to all kinds of relationships—family, friends, romantic relations, business partnerships, etc. People who have implemented this approach have seen the difference through a lighter life walk and less drama. It also helps us gain more self-confidence because we have more control of our environment and our state of mind.

Empathy as Part of the Equation

The keep-it-simple approach should focus on what is important for you and not for others. Sometimes, complexity arises from the drama around a decision, instead of the decision itself. As hard as it is, you must focus on the decision, not on the drama. It's your life, it's your choice, and it's your business—but you're not alone in the world. How you manage and communicate those decisions to the people around you is also important. Often, the empathy and love you added to that equation makes a difference. It's probably not going to change the outcome, but empathy helps to balance personal choices with a potential conflict or downturn in our relationships.

You should implement the keep-it-simple approach with empathy and care, avoiding a selfish and an individualistic line of thought. In the end, we are surrounded by people in different circles—family, social, work, etc. How we communicate our decisions could make a big difference. Not everyone will understand—nor do they have to understand—your dreams, goals, and mindset. So, it's on us to manage and communicate our decisions with empathy and kindness.

When my friends Mike and Jill got married, they decided what kind of ceremony they wanted. Like many engaged couples, they had several ideas about how they wanted that day to be. There were a lot of conversations about their wedding plans, including how many people, location, time, and budget. Mike and Jill decided they wanted to have an intimate and simple wedding and invite only the fifty people they really wanted to be with on that special day. They stuck to fifty guests, not because there was no flexibility but because they had a plan and worked toward it. The fifty-people goal encouraged them to think about who they really wanted to be with them on that day. It was a great exercise in setting priorities as a couple. But when Mike and Jill communicated their wedding plans to their inner circle, they received immediate pushback. They heard all kinds of comments.

"If you need money to invite more people, we can help,".

"How come you're not inviting your cousins?"

"That's not a wedding. That's a get-together."

"All that engagement time for a mini-wedding?"

It could've created conflict for other couples, but Mike and Jill were aligned on what they really wanted, so they expressed their view in a clear and honest way, and their point was understood, at least by the majority. While other couples in Mike and Jill's circle had big weddings and focused on the party, Mike and Jill focused on what was important and what really had value for them. For them, the value wasn't in the party, in a beach resort, or in a honeymoon in the Bahamas. The real value was that they were joining their lives forever and wanted to share the moment with their closest friends and family. Years later, Jill and Mike looked back and thought, *You know what? That was the right choice.*

As with many other decisions in life, their wedding didn't come without some collateral damage. Jill and Mike had to leave people out, people they appreciated. They made tough decisions. But that's no different from other choices in life, so Jill and Mike stuck to their goal and to what they had already visualized as a couple. That first big decision of their marriage was surrounded by conflict, opinions, and judgment—and that was good. That was the first test of character for their union. Their strategy was to address that big step with structure and stand behind their decision to have a very small, well-designed, and meaningful wedding event. The day was not about the party; it was about the mindset to start their journey together. And they kept it simple.

In summary, we can apply simplicity to all aspects of our lives, and it's directly related to focusing on the value-added factors of the life equation. This process also requires identifying and canceling the non-value-added factors. As with any other process, it takes time and self-discipline to develop a regular mindset. Simplicity leads to better decision-making and a more balanced life framework. Independently, it doesn't matter if it's a career decision (like whether to leave a job or accept an offer), a personal choice (like moving to a new location or ending a relationship), or a business decision (like determining the value of a business proposal). It's always better if you simplify the equation.

CHAPTER 7

YOUR PERSONAL ORGANIZATION

Organizations take the time to develop their vision, mission, and values as part of their strategic planning. They clearly define rules, roles, responsibilities, and processes for the team members. They also recognize achievements and address deviant conduct. All these factors create the culture of an organization.

Family is no different. Your family is your personal organization. Like any organization, family and personal relationships require leadership and a commitment to success. The family culture is shaped in a similar way. It doesn't just happen; we must cultivate it and work at it. Success at a family level is not a sales increase or profit growth at the end of the year. It's more about happiness, harmony, and fulfillment. It's about presence and a healthy coexistence. And this applies regardless of the family composition (family with kids, family with no kids, single parents, empty nesters, parents living with adult children, and so on). Your family is the most important team you can belong to. That is why it's important to give it the attention it needs. Addressing your most valuable team with a Life Management Approach can make a difference in a sometimes challenging coexistence.

Family is the foundation of society. It forms our views of the world, personal interactions, conflict management, and more. It all starts at home. Family culture is where values, traditions, general ideas, and an environment are created. It is also a child's first school of life. Some people don't see their family as a culture, but if you think about it, it's where all the basic behavior starts. It's in that inner circle where people shape what is right and wrong. That small culture is fundamental for individual development. We carry some of that early influence into adulthood. That's why the development of that small culture is important for the well-being of a couple, family, or any other relationship.

Family culture, like organizational culture, is not static. It can change due to several reasons, such as life events. Just as business organizations have policies and procedures, so do families. In that dynamic scenario, there's an opportunity to ask ourselves: What are our family values and policies? What internal practices can we improve? This is actually a good table topic exercise for couples.

The family culture or your "personal organization" is not created suddenly. You don't just wake up one day and say, "This is my family culture." You and all its members create it over time as a result of daily actions. It is in this inner circle, with everyone doing small things each and every day, where a solid foundation is created.

My family culture, as with every other culture, was not created overnight. It took years, conversations, and conflict management to get to the family culture we have today. Is it perfect? No, it's not. There is no such thing as a perfect culture. There are individual differences and discrepancies wherever there are human beings. Working on our family culture with defined core values and managing differences for the good of our organization and not just for the individual, helps us to achieve better levels of harmony in our daily lives.

My husband and I grew up in different countries and came from very different family cultures. Throughout the years, we decided to integrate the good things of each culture and work together to avoid the negative aspects from our previous environments. Family culture is a result of many factors, and the core values have a great influence on the overall family dynamic. Here are some examples of family core values:

Examples of Family Core Values

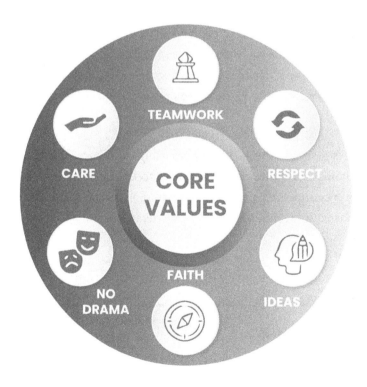

Teamwork

In a teamwork-oriented culture, the members help each other. This is a way to show love every day, by dividing the responsibilities with a high sense of engagement. Avoiding the "that is not my job" attitude and helping each other is a way to express love and care.

Respect

Respect in communication and respect for each other's time and space is very important. It's especially important when conflicts arise. Discrepancies are not solved with drama, raising our voices, or using foul language. And yes, these can be the first things that come to mind when we're angry. But when toxicity enters the equation, it becomes difficult to solve the issues or get to a solution. Most of us can pay attention and work with our behaviors to resolve issues by talking—and more importantly, listening to each other. Family issues must be resolved the same day to avoid starting a new day with drama. There is no issue worth hurting our loved ones with hostile words.

Care

Care is a simple thing that makes a big difference. "How is your day going? How was your day at school?" Looking into a loved one's eyes and asking a sincere question, with real connection, can increase our level of personal engagement.

No Drama

We should avoid drama, exaggeration, and victimization. It's not all about us.

Facts and Ideas

The dinner table plays a more important role than we might think. In any relationship, it's a great opportunity to sit together and share time every day. It is common to see one parent eating while on a business call, or a son having dinner while watching TV on the sofa. Dinner table conversation can impact the culture and environment of a family. It can strengthen family ties and should not be wasted talking about other people's lives and problems. Some people use the "no gossip" rule as part of the personal development effort of mind and soul clean up. If I can help, you can tell me. If I can't help, it's just gossip. Gossip is a completely useless activity It's not fun, and no, it's not entertainment. In the end, who am I to judge other people's lives? The time together should not be wasted talking about nonrelevant topics such as the daily politics or celebrity scandals.

Dinnertime is an excellent time to talk about facts, ideas, how the day was, or any topic relevant to the family's present reality. For example, relevant topics that stimulate conversation include latest school projects, new healthy dishes to try, daily fun facts, etc.

Faith

Integrating faith as a core value (regardless of beliefs) is another example of a core family value. The core values will be different in every family, just as they are different for each organization. What is important is to clearly define those values and integrate them in the execution, which is basically decisions and actions.

The Teamwork-Oriented Culture

John arrives home from a long workday. He goes to the living room, sits on the sofa, and turns on the TV to watch a sports game or his favorite series. He's having a well-deserved rest. His wife, Jane, also arrives home after a long workday. In her case, instead of going to sit on the sofa, she goes straight to the kitchen to make dinner. She also helps the kids with their homework and does laundry at the same time.

John has finished his workday, while Jane has started her second shift. Her first shift was working outside the home, and her second shift is the home tasks at the end of the day. This story repeats, day after day. All these tasks, in addition to other potential family stressors, can create an emotional burden for Jane. But no one talks about it because "that's just what moms and wives do." How do you think Jane feels? Does she feel happy and fulfilled? Maybe, but I wouldn't feel happy in her shoes. Not because of the kitchen or the laundry but because of a lack of engagement, care, and appreciation.

Let's look at this example in a **teamwork scenario**. John and Jane both come home tired from work. They both recognize that there are other tasks to do at home. As a team, they talk about it and identify the daily tasks. What is urgent, and what can wait, so they can finish and spend time together? Jane recognizes that she's not Wonder Woman and that everything doesn't have to be perfect. John proactively helps Jane with the necessary tasks because it's part of their daily routine.

In the background, the children observe, watching how the "house leaders" help each other with the little things—instead of Mom always begging for help, being in a bad mood, or staying up late to complete all the tasks by herself. Family teamwork requires balancing responsibilities and giving equal value to everyone's time. *If Dad can't be in the living room, let's help him so he can come to the living room with us, instead of watching him from our comfort zone.*

Just as they do in business, teams' relationship changes take time—time to improve or time to deteriorate. Teams can sometimes become complex and often have issues that prevent them from maximizing their performance. As with any other social system, they have their own identity, goals, and challenges. Successful teams don't just happen. They are a result of a combined effort by individuals with different backgrounds, sharing a common interest. Building up a successful team takes time and effort and requires leadership. This applies to organizations, but it also applies to our personal lives. There are models that provide different approaches for analyzing and improving teamwork. These models are based on the premise that teamwork is fundamental for the success of an organization. These models are not perfect but can help to create a mindset or a framework to manage our most important team. Let's take a look at how they can be integrated into a personal team.

The GRPI Model

GRPI stands for goals, roles, processes, and interpersonal relationships (Raue, et al. 2013). The model highlights the different aspects of teamwork, starting by identifying the main goals, followed by clarifying roles and responsibilities (R&Rs), and establishing processes and the interpersonal relationships of team members. Let's consider each in turn.

1. **Goals:** The foundation of any successful team starts with a clear goal definition. Goals provide direction and allow us to identify where the team is now and where the team aspires to be in the future. Most of the conflicts in teams arise from unclear goals, which can then cascade into unclear R&Rs and processes and negatively impact interpersonal relationships. Clear goals include acknowledgment and agreement of the desired results and expectations, priorities, and main tasks. Since this is the foundation of the approach, it's crucial to take time on the goals establishment process and address it with clarity, commitment, and honesty.

In the personal sense, establishing goals ensures that the team members (of any family composition) are looking in the same direction. That alignment comes with the integration of individual plans, dreams, and values. Successful teams are made up of people with different strengths, needs, and realities. The alignment and integration of each one to the common goal is what makes the difference.

2. **Roles and Responsibilities:** Team members should define and have a clear picture of who is doing what and of overall individual responsibilities. They should also agree on shared responsibilities and setting up clear boundaries. It is important to exercise this with a collaborative mindset and commitment. This part of the R&R definition includes the acceptance of team leadership, and sometimes, this can get complicated if it's not managed with a teamwork mindset. Some people may interpret this as a matter of power, when in fact, it is a matter of service and facilitation. Team leadership comes with work and responsibility. Family needs leadership in the same way businesses and organizations require leadership to be successful. Without leadership, there is no direction.

3. **Processes:** In this part of the model, the team defines how to make decisions, allocate resources, communicate, and manage conflicts that will arise sooner or later. The focus here is to determine how to maximize team interaction to support the common goals.

   Decision-making can be a point of inflection for any organization. As individuals, we must make small decisions, like what to eat today, and big decisions, such as a big investment or a career change. Decision-making can be stressful and create conflicts. In the same way as business organizations, personal teams should focus on the outcome and avoid drama as a key to get to a decision faster and more effectively.

Steven Covey, in his book *The Seven Habits of Highly Effective People,* shares a simple and interesting habit that I found valuable for keeping it simple and avoiding drama (Covey 2004). This habit assigns value on a scale for making decisions. For example: Person X and Person Y need to make a decision. From 1 to 10, how important is it to each of them? If X says it is a 9 and Y says it is a 3, it is done in the way of X. No energy is wasted on secondary things. Being honest and asking about the scale of values is showing respect for those who matter most to you. And if your happiness is tied to the other's happiness and achievements, it is a mutual benefit, even when your option is not favored. It's a type of democracy that shows respect for the power of feelings, and communication solves problems quickly.

Communication is the way team members share what they are doing and progress toward goals. In business, this could be regular tie-out calls or a common chat. Communication is essential for good decision-making. That's why team members should pay attention to communication styles and use all the positive tools possible, avoiding communication barriers. Communication barriers are anything that blocks or interferes with the message that someone is trying to send. These barriers can have a significant impact on personal and professional lives. Disengagement, lack of trust and clarity, poor frequency, and lack of active listening are examples of common communication barriers that can be harmful for our personal relationships.

In business and in life, we must also be aware that emotion can become a barrier to constructive communication. If you need to communicate with your team on sensitive subjects, it's important to do so in a sensitive way. The way you engage—including tone, body language, and your use of active listening—determines whether or not you invite constructive or effective dialogue.

4. **Interpersonal Relationships:** The fourth and final part of this model includes aspects like communication styles, trust, empathy, and flexibility. It also encompasses how members provide feedback to improve the team environment, and the level of collaboration to solve problems. Interpersonal relationships are highly impacted by the small things in daily interactions. And the good news is that almost all the things that can be done to improve it are free. Listen carefully, offer a "good morning," and treat others with good manners and kindness. Check to see if others need any help, keep your promises, and acknowledge your mistakes—all of these things are free and contribute to maintaining healthy relationships.

We might think we can't have a positive impact with our attitude, and that being polite is a weakness, but people will remember us by the way we treat them. All of these aspects, if applied in our personal lives, can bring positive results. Working to improve daily interactions can make a big difference in the quality of our personal relationships. Start focusing on yourself and on improving your mindset and your approach. Avoid making excuses such as "That's just how I am." This is the first step toward creating a better environment. It needs to start with you.

The Dysfunction Model

The dysfunction model establishes that all teams have the potential to be dysfunctional. To improve the performance of a team, it is important to understand the type and level of dysfunction. There are five potential levels of dysfunction in a team (Lencioni 2002).

1. **Absence of Trust:** The first disruption presented by this model happens when a team member doesn't want to acknowledge mistakes, weaknesses, or the need for help. These actions or attitudes influence the team environment and foundation. There needs to be a certain level of comfort within the team to create a good foundation. Trust is fundamental for the overall success of the team. Poor levels of trust will have a big impact on other important factors, such as decision-making and engagement.

2. **Fear of Conflict:** Engaging in debates is sometimes necessary to get to the root of an issue. Teams with poor foundations of trust don't have open and honest conversations. Without open and honest conversations, the debate to address an issue can turn into a worthless discussion or create a passive-aggressive environment (hostile comments, listening just to answer, and not really understanding each other). Poor debates lead to poor decision-making and may result in unsolved issues.

3. **Lack of Commitment:** Without proper solutions and agreements, it's difficult for a team to be committed to

results. Poor decisions create an environment of ambiguity and uncertainty. That's where we start to see answers like "I don't know who does that, but it's not me."

4. **Avoidance of Accountability:** Without commitment, even the best team player will hesitate to be engaged. This individual disengagement extends to the rest of the team, affecting performance and results. Disengagement can be dangerous, sometimes more dangerous than conflict. We can see it in our personal lives when people disengage from their families or relationships by making excuses like "I'm too busy" or just being emotionally absent from their loved ones. In our personal organizations, conflict can be unproductive, but disengagement can be sad.

5. **Inattention to Results:** If individuals don't focus on team results but rather focus on individual results, it's ultimately the business that suffers the consequences. In the personal organization, it is important to focus on ourselves but stay away from a selfish approach and integrate the value of synergy in our decisions and actions.

These five dysfunctions can be seen as a snowball that eventually leads to the failure of an organization. The impact of these dysfunctions can vary. It can lead to financial issues, high turnover, poor performance, or a company that's always in survival mode. This model, when applied to our personal lives, has a similar snowball effect. If we sit and analyze our surroundings, we will see these dysfunctions reflected somewhere. It's not our job to point a finger at the dysfunction of others, however. The value starts with analyzing ourselves and what kind of team players we are. Once we do that, the opportunity is in how we can conceptualize it, communicate it, and work over these dysfunctions to create a better environment and a more successful personal team.

Family Leadership Model

The real essence of leadership is service, not status or authority. I've seen how successful leaders present themselves as facilitators and not as authoritarian figures in their organizations. More than anything else, leaders are facilitators and problem solvers. But leaders must drive actions, and that will not always be well received by everyone. Sometimes leaders have to make tough decisions and will receive criticism and pushback. That's where things get hard and where the real leaders prove themselves.

The conflict of power is a common issue in organizations and is harmful for team performance. We all know the guy in the room that's always criticizing the leader, judging the leader's decisions, or minimizing the leader's style or character. In almost all cases, these are the ones that never come up with ideas or dare to make decisions because "it's not their job." Managing that kind of interaction is part of the leadership role. In our personal lives, there is also that guy in the room, and in these cases, the LMA is very useful. Address the situation with respect, without letting that person take control or feel dismissed, and focus on the results or on what really has value. This takes leadership skills, and it's something that can be developed. It's normal to be pissed off at the bad guy in the room, but once you work on these skills, you'll no longer be bothered.

Family leadership is no different from business leadership. Leaders have to make things happen and deal with all kinds of issues and pushback. That's why it's important to practice leadership with a service mindset. Family leadership is not about authority. It's about understanding goals and focusing on the guidance, service, and management of your inner circle's activities and resources.

The following teamwork model shows how the different factors integrate into a successful personal organization:

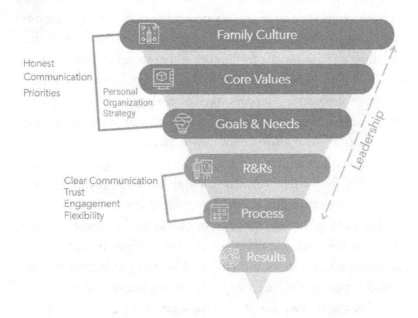

The success of any personal organization is not about perfection; it's about harmony and a healthy coexistence leading us to maintain deep and happy relationships. This reality does not happen overnight, it is cultivated daily through the small things that create a culture. As with any enterprise, the personal organization's culture is tied to its core values and goals, which are reflected in the "operations." The operations or execution are lined up by the roles, responsibilities, and processes. All these factors are aligned by the leadership and supported by the team members'

engagement. Trust and open communication are fundamental for any successful team.

While it is true that your family or any personal relationship is not a company, there are important aspects, like honest communication, looking in the same direction, clear R&R, and others mentioned in the chapter that can make a difference in your personal life. We must pay attention to how these factors manifest in our reality. This approach starts with you, as an individual. In the end, no one will knock on your door to offer you a happier family or more meaningful relationships. It's up to you to create or transform your personal organization, your most valuable team.

CHAPTER 8

FOLLOW YOUR STAR

It's easy to see why developing your personal organization is critical for developing a more fulfilling life, but an often-overlooked ingredient in the recipe of well-being is faith. It may seem contradictory how God would fit into a book titled *The Strategic Business of You*. For some, God and business are not compatible because a business could be a self-served item, something completely mundane and materialistic. But God gave us the gift of life and free will, and it is on each of us to embrace that gift with the responsibility and the value it deserves. No one is going to live and act for you. It's your deal, your life, and your business.

The life management concepts applied in previous chapters have the goal of helping us to achieve a more meaningful, joyful, and genuine life. So how is faith related to these concepts? Faith is that intangible element in the equation that leads to results through calmness and strength—the strength to manage creative destruction, to define our needs, and to work on our SWOT and 80/20. Faith ultimately helps us to act within the LMA and to execute our personal plan. Faith is also fundamental in facing adversity. Aligning faith to the LMA is a way to honor the gift of life in every minute of every day, in our choices and actions.

The presence of God in my life equation has been real and fundamental in a human sense. That connection to God is manifested through thoughts, intentions, and actions. Working on my thoughts to keep in mind what God wants from me helps me to align my intentions and is eventually reflected in my decision-making process. I am always asking Him for help and the gift of discernment. It is not about feigning perfection or pretending to be morally or spiritually superior. It is about walking the path, following His light, and listening to His voice.

Books have changed my perspectives, my views, and my mindset toward life and decision-making. They have shown me a lot about others—real people with real struggles and tragedies, humans just like me, who have overcome adversity, many of them with God in their equation. It might sound silly or naïve, but God has been with me in all my sunshine, storms, and deserts—and he has always shown me the path.

The purpose of faith in the Life Management Approach is not to assign a religious hierarchy or to preach one way of experiencing the divine. For you, that may be through one organized religion or another. It may be through faith or in a higher power. I encourage you to consider this chapter with an open mind and an open heart, to take from it what speaks to you.

Show Me the Path: Integration of the God Factor

It was a hot summer evening in the late nineties. My family and I were waiting for my father to come back home after a work trip. It was Sunday. After getting a call from the police, we traveled to a distant police station to get the terrible news that my father had died. I had just turned seventeen the week before. At that moment, I felt the world turn around. I had lost the protective figure who, all my life, had made me feel that everything was going to be fine. I was so shocked at that moment that I couldn't even cry. I looked at the sky full of stars, and I thought, *God, I am not one to ask why. I only ask you to show me the path. Please don't leave us alone.*

The grief captured our house in the following days. We were completely isolated in our sadness. By then, there were no more tears in my eyes, and for the first time in my life, I felt the silence of the soul.

A few weeks after my father died, a big hurricane hit, leaving our town and house without water and power for weeks. Those were times of so much sadness and darkness, literally. But even in the middle of the fear, loneliness, and uncertainty, I always felt that God was there with me. He never left. One day, I asked my mom what we would do from then on. Her response to my question was clear and simple. "I don't have all the answers," she said. "I just know that God does not abandon anyone—God does not abandon *anyone.*" Decades after, I understood that Mom couldn't have been more right.

In the following years, especially in the last decade, I've focused on seeking God beyond a temple, which I think is also very important, but I needed to find Him inside me, in my daily life, in my tribulations and difficulties. Seeking that personal relationship with God helped me to embrace Him in my day-to-day life and in my choices.

Growing up in a Christian family, religion was part of our culture. We used to gather for all the important Christian celebrations, like Lent, Christmas, and Easter. At some point, I felt that

God was there, but was out there and not actively inside of me. That's when I felt the need to bring the relationship to a deeper level—an authentic level in which He is with me every minute, every hour, in my decisions, in my whole equation, not only part of it. I wanted to feel His presence in a realistic way and not in an idealistic way. I wanted to bring the relationship out of the church and not attach it to a single place or only to Sundays. To do that, I understood that I had to call Him, I had to seek Him, and I had to hear Him.

The figure of the Three Kings helped me in the "how to" process. They were three wise men, from distant lands. I think they were busy in their daily lives, but they stopped what they were doing to follow a sign. Maybe they seemed crazy or foolish at that time for following a star. But they moved, they sought, and they found Him in an unexpected place. And when they found Jesus at the stable, they didn't just pray and say, "Let's get back to work." The Three Kings had a very personal connection with Jesus by adoring Him and offering their gifts. Just like the Three Kings, our life is a walk. We should watch for the signs, look for our Star, and listen to God, who speaks to us in different ways.

Follow Your Star

Reading books and articles about spiritual growth is helpful to expand your perspective by seeing how others have tied their faith to their daily lives. There is too much content directed to different audiences. I recommend trying to select more centered content, staying away from extreme influences. Expanding your knowledge will help to acquire a better interpretation of God's message, and how messages from holy texts like the Bible or others integrate into life and the modern world. And I'm not talking about doing a biblical dissertation. It is about the content we consume; it's about feeding or watering our minds with information that helps in the expansion and strengthening of spiritual well-being.

Praying is also an important part of the God factor. As our heavenly Father, he listens and he answers. Even after some time, we may think He is not listening, but that constant connection, even if it's brief, is very important. One example of that communication could be integrating personal prayer or reading time into your family culture. It could be through Bible reading or family prayer at night. Nothing rigorous, and not as a ritual, but as a daily one-on-one with the Lord at the end of each day. You can also opt for guided meditation or spend time reflecting on things you are grateful for. Praying together or engaging in other mindfulness acts has been a tool to connect with the most important aspect of our lives daily. In a world full of distractions, it can be challenging to call, hear, and seek. Praying is one great way to establish that connection.

Another important aspect is developing and integrating meekness in the thought process. **Meekness** can be seen as weakness, but it ends up being the opposite because it is a real manifestation of character. It is not a perfect recipe for how to act but rather a mindset acquired over time as a result of reflection about life. It involves the observation of how we react in some circumstances, observing how others act, and learning from them. The process is not to judge who is right or wrong; it is to help improve personal development and decisions. This approach helps me not to feel the need to always respond or have the last word. And it's not about being quiet. It's about reducing the urge to fight worthless battles. In other words, listen to understand and not to argue.

Have you ever met someone who is always in a "conflictive" mode? Someone who's always offended or always talking about fights with a coworker, their boss, an ex, or a customer? Many people who live in a conflictive mode have one factor in common: stagnation. Conflictive mode becomes a habit that takes us away from the 20 percent concept shared in previous chapters. Also, it fills the head and the heart with unnecessary noise. Although most of us have been exposed to conflict or have disagreements with others, there is no need to live in the wheel of conflict, where battles are always present.

Some of the best leaders I have met in my career had in common the ability not to jump into meaningless discussions. To some, they might look weak, but at the end of the day, they were the doers, not the talkers. Meekness helps me to ignore the pointless noise, better integrate empathy and humbleness in my relationships with others, and focus on what is really important. The application and development of the virtue of meekness is aligned to the concept of 20 percent. It helps me walk lightly by taking out the non-value-added things and focusing on the important things that bring joy and meaning to life.

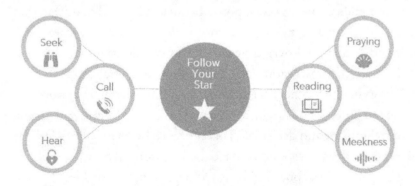

I can tell you honestly that the God factor has materialized in my life equation, and the same can happen in your life equation. Reading helps to interpret his message and integrate it into decision-making. Prayer keeps the connection by presenting intentions, projections, and fears, and being grateful for all that we have. Meekness helps us focus on what really has value and rejecting emotional trash. These aspects can be applied to strengthen the spiritual pillar, as it takes time until it flows automatically. Incorporating faith—in whatever form that takes for you—so that it is always present will make a difference and can help you move to a better version of yourself.

CHAPTER 9

CHOICES

As we've explored the umbrella that is the Life Management Approach, we've considered many elements that add up to create a more meaningful life. The final piece of this puzzle is perhaps the most important one. Have you already guessed it? That's right. It's all about choices.

I have been repeating this to myself a lot in my adult life. Life is about decisions, like it or not. Sometimes this phrase has slapped me in my face; sometimes it has helped me make hard decisions. You choose your networks, your job, the digital content you consume, what you eat, your partner, and a lot of other things. Your life is a cluster of small and big decisions.

And yes, as I mentioned in other chapters, there are things you don't choose. You don't have full control over all things that happen in life, which is sometimes full of adversity. You don't choose to lose a loved one, your job, or your business. You don't choose to be betrayed or have a disease impact a loved one. But you can choose how to address those things and what you do with the experience.

The difference is in how you navigate those difficult times and what you from them—or how you grow from the things that happen to you that you cannot control. Maybe you already see this statement in hundreds of self-development books, or it might sound like a cliché, but I've adapted this to my life to prove that how you react to adversity is a choice.

The fact is very simple. We live on planet Earth. This is not Heaven. Not only is this not Heaven, but we live in a world full of distractions and invitations to make bad choices, or simply not take action and go with the flow. We must pay attention to our inner selves; to our own business because success, happiness, and inner peace don't just show up in life. A better career or a good relationship are not going to knock on your door while you watch sports or a TV series. You can create a better reality with structure and consistency. I would say we must become obsessed with that goal if we want a better life.

Early in my career, a boss once gave me a task. "This sounds like a big deal and a good opportunity," I said. "How am I going to do it?"

"Well, you'll have to figure out the 'how' for this or any other task in business," he answered. "You have to make things happen."

I think that was a great lesson, and I've also applied it to life. I have a task, a dream, or a goal. I don't know how to do it. But I have to make things happen. It's no one else's task. It's my duty.

The Harvest

Our choices have an impact. They can impact the short and the long term. We can visualize the process as a harvest: (1) prepare and clean the ground or soil, (2) select the seed, (3) plant the seed, (4) wait, (5) harvest. We must pay attention to each of these steps. If we don't prepare and clean the soil, select the best seed possible, work on the planting process, and apply the right watering, how do you think the harvest will be? If we just want immediate gratification or we don't want to be patient, we probably know what we're going to get.

It's very tempting just to live in the harvest without working on the process of cleaning and preparing the ground and doing all the planning and execution, which often require discipline and hard work. People who want to live in the harvest are probably the ones that look at others' harvest with some resentment. "Oh, they have a better harvest every season because they are lucky, have more resources, or have better soil." These people get creative with excuses. They don't acknowledge that they didn't pay attention to the soil or their seeds. They don't admit that they could've done a better job.

The same applies to our lives. This harvest analogy can be implemented in the decision-making process for business or life by following these steps: (1) gather information, (2) decide, (3), act, (4) adjust and improve, (5) repeat. Let's take a look at each of these steps in greater detail.

1. **Gather Information:** This step is like the ground-preparation process. The data will not provide the answer, but it will get us closer to the answer. When I talk about decisions, I always emphasize that we made the choice with the information available at that particular moment. Later

analysis is always easier because after the fact, you will probably have the full picture. In business or in your personal life, the ground-preparation process is about ideas: to clear our minds and have information that helps us to make the best choice possible.

Gathering information includes accessing relevant content that helps in the decision-making process, such as books, educational videos, consultants, and so on. When I started my company, I looked for expert advice. I sought out consulting experts, legal counsel, tax advisors, and online marketing experts. All the conversations and consultations had the objective of gathering as much available information as possible to take action. Those experts were not going to tell me what I should do with my company, but learning from their experience would help me make my own decisions. Even if something were to go wrong, at least I had tried to make informed decisions. As another example, after his divorce, one of our close friends identified that he needed to pay more attention to managing his finances, retirement, and household expenses. He decided to educate himself about these topics—not to become an expert but to integrate the learning into his personal decisions rather than just make decisions without exploring other outlooks.

A lot of things we're living through have been other people's experiences before. Hearing about how they addressed those experiences can give us a line of sight in our decision process. We can take advantage of those experiences, not to live our lives as others do but to expand our perspective, with a goal of making better choices.

2. **Decide:** This is similar to the process of selecting a seed. It's when you know what direction you're going in or what you really want. You have a clear view of the next step, and you're ready to act.

When my business partners Leo and Ann bought their first house, they had different likes and needs, so they sat down together and made a list of preferences. They listed the features they wanted and didn't want in their house and what was important to each of them, such as neighborhood, price range, and internal layout. On the initial list, everything was needed, and nothing was negotiable. After making that first list with so many different items on it, they drilled down to the ones that were "good to have" versus what they "must have." Both Leo and Ann had to make trade-offs. Through elimination and negotiation, they simplified the list, and this helped the realtor in the market search. The exercise took a few conversations. They left out the drama and constantly reminded themselves of the common goal. It was a couple's decision, a team choice. The result was a clear expectation on what they wanted for their next house.

3. **Act:** When we have all the information and know what we want, it's time to act. It's time to plant the seed. Action is the end result of the thought process, idea, and information gathering. A decision without action is just an intention. Actions don't have to be radical. Sometimes we'll have to take big steps, but a lot of results come from small actions over time.

Like any project, execution or implementation is the hardest part. It's when all the fears invade us, where we find the issues and complexity of the real stuff. Sometimes you'll feel that you're in the middle of a storm. You may ask yourself, "Who told me to do this?" But this is exactly when you should stay focused on your end goal. This is where you apply the 80/20 rule, focusing on the 20 percent of the actions that produces 80 percent of the results.

4. **Adjust and Improve:** In this step, we evaluate the result of our decisions and execution. It is like evaluating the harvest process. Many times, we must wait years to evaluate results. Other times, we can evaluate the results of the process in the short term. The important point is that this becomes a process of *introspection* and *self-evaluation*. The development and growing process is an iterated process that requires review and improvement.

In this part, we should allow ourselves flexibility under a structured framework. Lack of flexibility can add an unnecessary emotional burden in the decision-making process. While staying away from any mediocre approach, we should not ask ourselves for perfection because if we do that, there's a chance we will end up not acting. Previously, I talked about kindness and empathy, and we shouldn't forget about ourselves when we think of kindness and empathy. Also, we should allow ourselves the time and space to recharge, reconnect, and reevaluate next steps. What we see as a failure or a closed door today could be an opportunity or open door tomorrow.

5. **Repeat:** Moving toward a more meaningful life with the Life Management Approach is not a one-time effort. It becomes a repetitive process of visualization, an establishment of needs, values, goals, available resources, and

priorities—and in the end, action. The repetition becomes a cycle through a new mindset that supports action. These actions are not final; it's an endless process that is sometimes more active or aggressive, and other times more passive and smaller.

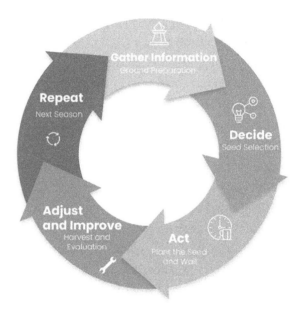

There is not always time for a well-structured decision-making process. And we don't have to go through a full process to choose if we want soup or salad for lunch. It's about the conceptualization of ideas prior to a choice focused on values, needs, resources, and goals. In summary, it's about making choices based on what is really important.

A Bad Harvest

Sometimes you do your due diligence, and you still don't have a good harvest. You don't get a good result, or everything turns out the opposite of what you expected. That's part of the game. Throughout the whole process, there may be things that go wrong. Sometimes it can be external factors. Or sometimes we may have ignored internal factors or just didn't see them at the moment we took action. All big things have a risk factor in the equation, and winning requires a certain level of tolerance of failure. The important part of failure is learning and trying to figure out what went wrong to avoid it in the future.

You can follow the guidelines, and there's still a chance you'll get a bad product, harvest, or result. Is that a failure? Not necessarily. A lot of times, things just don't go as we expected, but we can choose how we manage it. We can drop the ball, complain, and blame others. Or we can approach it with a creative-destruction mindset, take it as a bad harvest or a bad season, try to understand what went wrong, and move on.

Of course, we all want the best harvest, and we should work to get the best results. But seeking perfection can wear us down, and we may end up doing nothing. If you failed, at least you tried. You can adjust, improve, or try again. Often, the fear of failure is one of the major roadblocks. The good news is that if we can manage our fear, we can overcome that roadblock and move forward.

The Choice of Discipline

The word discipline is sometimes seen as painful or as punishment; it can sound extremely rigid or controlling. But we must see discipline as a gift to ourselves. If we address life with discipline—discipline with our time, our body, our money, and our relationships—we will see a better outcome. The structure you apply to your life and your decisions will take you to a better result or will help you to "make it happen."

Addressing life with structure and discipline is possible. It's just a matter of starting to make small changes that will become big changes. There are different techniques, depending on the goal. If your goal is to have better health or better finances, you can use different techniques, but in the end, all of these strategies and concepts are aligned with structure and discipline.

The fundamental part of a disciplined mindset is action. We can think, dream, or make the best plan for a better life. The important thing is how we translate all that into actions. Discipline can be the difference between success and failure. Intelligence without discipline won't get us very far. I've known a lot of really smart people with excellent grades and good retention and intelligence who've had completely unsuccessful, unbalanced, and unhappy lives. Some of them made all kinds of bad decisions that impacted their physical and mental health, their careers, and their relationships. In almost all cases, one of the common factors was a lack of discipline, order, structure, and thought clarity.

No one is in your shoes, but in a large way, you choose your shoes. Looking for a more meaningful life is not about regretting what you haven't done or feeling sorry about decisions from the past. It's about looking forward, always looking for the next season, regardless of how early or late you are in life. Every day is a new opportunity. With every sunrise, we have a chance to embrace it as the beginning of our next harvest season. How you address the next season, that's your choice. Remember the iterative process required to make choices and commit to the steps that will get you to the end result you desire.

CONCLUSION

We all know of successful companies that have reinvented themselves and are now leaders. Some of these companies were in very bad shape before they turned around. To reinvent themselves, those companies reviewed their vision, changed their strategies, launched a plan, maximized opportunities, allocated resources toward a new direction, and executed. Some of these companies' decisions were more drastic than others, but in the end, they took risks and acted instead of giving up and blaming the market or other external factors. These turnarounds take a lot of analysis, discussion, and hard choices in a structured way.

In your life, you may have also experienced setbacks that have left you questioning whether it's worth the effort it takes to try again. Maybe you've made all the "right choices" but were still left feeling dissatisfied or unfulfilled. Whatever your experience, the LMA will give you the structure that'll lead to reinvention—but this time, not for a company. This time, it is for ourselves.

To achieve balance between the four pillars of well-being—physical, emotional, spiritual, and financial—reflect on the models presented in this book:

Through **creative destruction**, we make the best of the worst. Look for personal reinvention, even in adversity, through personal innovation and reengineering. Consider your **pyramid of needs,** which can help you align your personal needs with your individual values and your vision for the future. And don't forget to use your personal **SWOT** to maximize opportunities through growth and self-development.

Ultimately, the Life Management Approach is about the best possible allocation of our most valuable resources (time, energy, and money). It's also about exercising prioritization with discipline, looking for the 20 percent, and simplifying the equation. **The 80/20** approach focuses on the value assignment of individual resources, paying particular attention to time management as part of your personal operational model and recognizing the value of energy. The **simplification process** helps you manage what can become a very complex life equation. In this simplification process, we identify and assign more weight to some variables and cancel others that steal from us or attempt to work against our most valuable resources.

Looking into the action level, the LMA helps us execute in a new framework, which starts with us and our closest relationships. Understanding that our families and those closest to us are our most valuable team and allocating our resources accordingly is important for what I call our **personal organization.** Having God in the equation—or **following your Star**—also makes a big difference on how we execute and how we manage adversity. These elements are fundamental for the emotional and spiritual pillars.

Success is about working in balance and harmony to have the best harvest possible. And if you have a bad harvest, move on and look forward to the next season. Money, recognition, and other things are just a result. These things should not be the driver and are not an indicator of success—real success. Focus instead on the **choices** that will get you where you want to be.

Discipline is a very important part of the LMA. We should embrace it as a gift to ourselves and not as self-punishment. It is a tool that drives action. Discipline helps you allocate your most valuable resources—time, energy, and money—toward your dreams and goals.

LIFE MANAGEMENT APPROACH

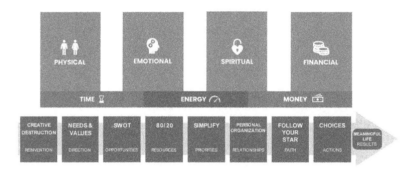

The development of the Life Management Approach or a new mindset is like any other improvement process. You don't get a diploma in one week; you don't get fit in one month; your investments don't give you a good return in a short period of time. It all takes time and perseverance to reinvent and give better structure to our lives. Unlike a company, life is not about revenue or what we can get from others. It's about giving the best of ourselves to ourselves. Only then can we share our best with others, and that's where the real significance is—when we share our true and best results with the world. We are our most important business and our most important job. Your most important business is the business of you.

REFERENCES

Covey, Stephen R. 2004. *The 7 Habits of Highly Effective People: Powerful Lessons in Personal Change*. New York: Free Press.

Lencioni, Patrick. 2002. The Five Dysfunctions of a Team: A Leadership Fable. Hoboken: Jossey-Bass.

McLeod, Saul. 2023. "Maslow's Hierarchy of Needs." Simply Psychology.

Nevshehir, Noel. 2021. "How to Ensure the Benefits of 'Creative Destruction' Are Shared by All." World Economic Forum, Entrepreneurship.

Raue, Steve, Suk-Han Tang, Christian Weiland, and Claas Wenzlik. 2013. *The GRPI Model: An Approach for Team Development*. Berlin: Systemic Excellence Group.

Schumpeter, Joseph A. 1950. *Capitalism, Socialism, and Democracy*. New York: Harper Perennial.

Tartell, Ross. 2016. "Understand Teams by Using the GRPI Model." Training Magazine.

Tardi, Carla. 2022. 80-20 Rule. Investopedia.

Printed in the USA
CPSIA information can be obtained
at www.ICGtesting.com
LVHW100820290124
769705LV00004B/487